"Do miracles happen today?

"There can be no doubt after reading *Heroes of the Holocaust*. Each of these heroes, these fortunate survivors, experienced miracles of compassion, humanity, and yes, divine intervention.

"Why were these spared so miraculously? Only God knows the answer to that—but we can still be moved to hope and gratitude as we read *Heroes of the Holocaust*."

—Pat Boone

HEROES
of the
HOLOCAUST

Arnold Geier

ILLUSTRATIONS
T.G. Friedman

INTRODUCTION
Abraham H. Foxman

Berkley Books, New York

HEROES OF THE HOLOCAUST

A Berkley Book / published by arrangement with
the author

PRINTING HISTORY
Londonbooks edition published 1993
Berkley trade paperback edition / February 1998

The Putnam Berkley World Wide Web site address is
http://www.berkley.com

ISBN: 0-425-16029-7

BERKLEY®
Berkley Books are published by The Berkley Publishing Group, a
member of Penguin Putnam Inc., 200 Madison Avenue, New York,
New York 10016.
BERKLEY and the "B" design
are trademarks belonging to Berkley Publishing Corporation.

Contents

Author's Preface

Heroes of the Holocaust focuses on stirring, remarkable stories of people helping people survive in a society bent on genocide. Often, rescue depended on individuals making crucial decisions at a moment's notice, based on their personal sense of values and without regard to their own personal safety. To some degree, the results support Anne Frank's assertion that "in spite of everything, people are really good at heart."

It was not until 1984 that I was able to relate my personal story (see "Broken Glass, Broken Lives" and "From Darkness to Light") to anyone, including my own sons. That spring, my wife and I took advantage of a rare opportunity to visit the Falashas, the black Jews of Ethiopia, in the hills of Gondar Province of that long-isolated land. We were inspired by the tenacity and courage with which they had held on to their religion for almost 3,000 years, believing themselves to be the only Jews on earth. Our small group of adventurers met for a final drink on the terrace of the Addis Ababa Hilton and, enraptured with awe and admiration for the successful endurance of the Ethiopian Jews, the group's leader told his personal story of survival during the European Holocaust. It was a tale of wonder, hope and inspiration. The intense interest of the group encouraged me to tell mine, with similar results. That night, I pledged myself someday to chronicle for future generations the remarkable stories of acts of human kindness, of extraordinary courage or "miracles" that had helped people to survive the Holocaust. After three years and over 200 interviews and submissions from all over the world, I selected and wrote the twenty-eight poignant stories of *Heroes of the Holocaust*.

For decades, many survivors were simply unable to talk about their experiences—it was too painful. I could see the anguish in their faces and hear it in their voices as I interviewed them and shared their pain. Often, they released streams of tears and, with them, some of the emotions they had pent up for many years. They realize that they are the last witnesses and that their stories will die with them unless recorded now.

Unfortunately, it has become necessary to counteract the brazen attacks of those who now deny that the Holocaust ever occurred. It is also vital that we teach future generations that individuals can make the difference between good and evil. The library shelves should contain at least some reference that, on occasions, rays of light penetrated the sinister darkness which enveloped humanity. Anne Frank asserted the basic nature of humanity. This book proves the wisdom of her belief in absolute terms. Here are heartwarming, true tales of real heroes in action.

—ARNOLD GEIER
Miami, Florida

Commentary

by Rabbi Harold M. Schulweis

In a world inundated by stories and episodes of violence, betrayal and xenophobia, the evidence of contemporary moral heroism deserves to be high on the agenda of the post-Holocaust civilization. Our children cry out for models of behavior that uplift and sustain faith in ourselves and in our neighbors.

Mr. Geier has masterfully presented the peak experiences of flesh and blood persons, ordinary people, whose consciences demanded that they do not succumb to the falsehood that there is no alternative to passive complicity with evil.

The testimony presented in this book is a gift of hope. It speaks of intrigues of good people for the rescue of the persecuted, of collusions of conspiracy for the sake of protecting the hounded, of nuns and priests and convents and people who made of themselves hiding places for the persecuted.

These are the holy subterfuges which altruistic men and women have used to help the damned.

I commend this book for old and young people alike, for Jews and Gentiles, for those who need the heart to believe again. Without such memories, life is emptied of meaning.

—RABBI HAROLD M. SCHULWEIS, Chairman
Jewish Foundation for Christian Rescuers/ADL

Heroes of the Holocaust
From a Historic Perspective

Jewish misfortunes did not begin in Germany with the rise of Adolf Hitler. For centuries, the country had harbored strong anti-Jewish feelings. However, they were intensified in the Nazi era until they erupted in a frenzy of brutality and genocide unequaled in the annals of modern history.

The Jews had lived in Germany for over 2,000 years. Originally, they came with the conquering Roman Legions and settled into peaceful and fruitful lives in their communities. All that changed, beginning with the Crusades in the 11th century. European Christians, propelled by religious convictions, became hostile to the Jews because they refused to accept Christ as the Messiah. This often resulted in violence, massacres and expulsions. Forced conversions became routine. After the Church prohibited Christians from charging interest, it left to the Jews the money lending business so vital to commerce. Ironically, this provided an additional incentive to hate the Jews who seemingly made profit from Christians in a parasitic way. In some cases, killing a Jew eliminated a creditor under the guise of religious zealotry. Jews, forced to live in ghettos, were isolated from the Christians and became easily accessible for acts of violence.

The Black Death epidemic in 1340–1351 was blamed on the Jews, and their persecution increased. Eventually, most Germanic Jews fled to the east and formed communities in what are now Poland, Russia, Belorus, Ukraine, Romania, Hungary, Lithuania, Latvia, Slovakia and the Czech Republic.

It was not until the early 1800s that the remaining Jews in Germany were let out of the ghettos and were gradually allowed to integrate into German society. By 1880, they had achieved full and equal citizenship under the nation's law.

Feeling comfortable with being German, the Jews contributed significantly in public service, commerce, education, the arts, science and medicine. But many Germans refused to accept them as fellow citizens. Following their tradition of centuries of religious and economic hostilities, they blamed Jews for whatever hardships the nation encountered. Despite the equality guaranteed them by law, few Jews reached positions of influence and power in the upper ranks of government, the military and education.

After World War I, Germany, under the terms of the Versailles Treaty which imposed enormous reparations and losses of territory, experienced a period of chaos, revolution, economic disaster and national humiliation. Extremists carried anti-Semitism one step further by declaring Jews to be a sinister race, and blamed them for all of Germany's misfortunes. They called for the expulsion of Jews from German society, and their views received increasing acceptance by the rest of the population.

Adolf Hitler joined a rowdy group of ruffians, the Nazis (National Socialists), who espoused racial anti-Semitism and looked upon the Jew as evil incarnate. Needing a scapegoat, they deflected public anger at the prevailing critical social and economic turmoil toward the Jews. So receptive were the German people to these concepts that they gave the Nazis power in the elections of 1933.

Racial anti-Semitism became national policy. As a separate race, Jews could be isolated from others around them. Immediate steps were taken to eliminate them from public life. Workers in government, education and medicine were dismissed. In 1935, special laws were passed declaring Jews to be second-class citizens, prohibiting their marriage to Germans and limiting social and business contacts between Jews and Germans. These laws ennobled former extremist theory to accepted fact.

During the night of November 9–10, 1938, Nazis all over Germany burned synagogues, plundered Jewish businesses and raided Jewish homes, arresting over 30,000 Jewish men. Some were deported to the Polish border, while others were sent to concentration camps, established to confine criminals and political prisoners, in Dachau, Buchenwald and Sachsenhausen. It was the clearest revelation of Germany's intent to rid itself of Jews.

Initially, the government wanted to harass its Jews and make it impossible for them to earn a living, in hopes that many would simply leave. Most Jews of Germany and Austria, which was annexed by Hitler in March 1938, saw the proverbial handwriting on the wall.

Many, with relatives in other lands, were able to obtain the appropriate papers and left legally. Others sought refuge in countries—any that would accept them—all over the world, but most were refused entry. There was a global economic depression and no one was eager to admit people who would compete for scarce jobs or become a burden on the state. Other German Jews were reluctant to leave the country for which they had fought, where their ancestors had lived for centuries and to which they had pledged their allegiance. Of approximately 800,000 Jews in Germany and Austria, 450,000 left or escaped before the Nazis plunged the world into war.

With the occupation of Poland in 1939, the Nazis acquired over 1.8 million more Jews, descendants of those who had fled the Germanic areas centuries earlier. These Jews remained segregated from their Christian neighbors, spoke a language (Yiddish) similar to medieval German, dressed in traditional garb and practiced their religious rituals. Under the Russian Czar until the end of World War I, they were restricted to specified districts. Considered second-class citizens, they were often attacked and brutalized. In the independent Poland after World War I, popular feelings of prejudice continued against them.

The Nazis realized that the policy of driving Jews out of the area could not work. In one military action, they found themselves with more unwanted Jews than they originally had in their own country. Once the war began, there were no other lands into which to drive them. So they began to herd the Jews into ghettos, governed by appointed or elected Jewish Councils to keep order in the run-down quarters and enforce all Nazi edicts.

With every German conquest, there were more Jews. The Nazis, who had set out to eliminate Jews from their society, were collecting them in record numbers. At first, they were forced into slave labor and allowed to die from hunger and disease. But when Hitler planned the attack on the Soviet Union, with its millions of Jews, it was decided to systematically eliminate all the Jews of Europe.

As German troops advanced in the east, special units, led by Nazi officers and often manned by local volunteers, rounded up all Jews, forced them to dig trenches, then shot and buried them in the graves they had just completed. By early 1942, they had murdered about 1.4 million men, women and children.

But shooting was not efficient enough by German standards. They built death camps, with gas chambers and ovens to kill and dispose of the victims. At a conference called in January 1942 in the Berlin suburb of Wannsee, a transportation network was organized to bring trainloads of Jews and other "undesirables" directly to the death factories. The first camp was erected in Chelmno, Poland, in 1941. Others followed at Belzec, Treblinka, Auschwitz, Sobibor and Majdanek, to mention a few of the most notorious ones. From then on, when they became too ill or exhausted to work, Jews from labor camps all over Europe were shipped to the death camps. Ghettos were systematically liquidated, structures burned to the ground, their occupants shipped to camps. Jews from occupied and allied countries were rounded up, often with the enthusiastic assistance of local authorities, and transferred to the gas chambers. These included men, women and children in Croatia, Greece, Czechoslovakia, Hungary, Romania, Jugoslavia, Italy, Holland, Belgium, France, Luxembourg, Estonia, Latvia and Lithuania. It is estimated that about 5.8 million Jews perished at the hands of the Nazis and their collaborators.

At first, the Germans avoided resistance by deception and tricks to veil their intentions. Usually, the victim went along with "resettlement" to a labor camp or "transfer" to another area, not realizing that all Nazi roads led to the gas chambers. At first, Jews were not even aware of the death camps. But, in addition to the few individuals who escaped and joined Partisan units, there were heroic insurgencies. These included revolts by the Jews of the Polish town Czestochowa, in the Treblinka and Sobibor death camps, and the historic Warsaw ghetto uprising in April 1943, which defied large German units for almost a month. In each instance, Nazi forces overwhelmed the poorly equipped, emaciated and grossly outnumbered rebels.

There were other noteworthy acts of resistance. When the people of Denmark learned of the impending deportation of their Jewish friends and neighbors, they organized their fishing fleet to spirit their fellow citizens to sanctuary in Sweden. Almost all of the 7,000 Danish Jews were saved. In Bulgaria, an ally of Germany, the government, with the support of the Church and the people, stopped deportation of its Jewish citizens, in defiance of Nazi wishes. In France and Belgium, over half the Jews were saved, most by hiding with friends, strangers and in convents, or with forged documents. In Hungary, Raoul Wallenberg, the Swedish diplomat, saved thousands of Jews by declaring them to be under his government's protection.

There were a precious few who extended a hand of hope to those drowning in the sea of death and despair. Although their numbers were comparatively infinitesimal, they must not be forgotten. This is not only as a matter of honor, justice and decency, but also to help us confront our feelings.

A reflection upon the Holocaust leads to anger, rage and a feeling of impotence. So many human beings died, so few were saved, and so little was done to help them. We need the stories of rescue, self-sacrifice, righteousness and morality to begin a process of healing. They can never balance the unrelenting story of evil, yet they exemplify the goodness that often lies within man. When asked why they helped, most rescuers responded, "It was the right thing to do." Their acts were the results of upbringing, religious and moral convictions, and opportunity.

They suddenly found themselves in a position to help. They did not consider themselves heroes but human beings who confronted a situation with the response most natural to them. "They had nowhere to go, so I took them in," explained the French woman who, at the risk of her life, harbored a small family for months.

Heroes of the Holocaust

An Introduction

by Abraham H. Foxman

The surprising aspect of this collection of stories from the Holocaust years is the number of times Jews appeared to have been helped by their Christian neighbors. These stories do not exculpate or ignore the sinister behavior of most Europeans (by far) who supported Nazis. Against a backdrop of vast documentation elsewhere expressing Europe's moral failure, these stories help explain why some Jews survived.

We learn, for example, about a Polish physician who risked his life to provide false identity papers for Bianca Perlmutter. From a doctor we would hope for kindness like this. But historians have recently shown the racial bias of "Nazi doctors." *This* physician was obviously different. He enabled Bianca to live, less by dint of training than by his unshakable humanity.

Another remarkable story describes the courage of a member of the French resistance. Conducting a train, he spirited Louise Abouaf and her mother from Nazi aggression. This, too, we would expect from a Nazi despiser, but numerous accounts show how anti-Semitism imbued the Resistance and the Partisans. Here again we're impressed by *individual* courage that springs ultimately from irreducible kindness.

My own story illustrates the point. Abundant historical evidence has implicated Poles in the demise of European Jewry. Indeed, the Jewish community feels rage to this day. But that's too simplistic. Though understandable, it would be nobler to refrain from delivering such indictments of collective guilt. Stories of kindness by Poles—many presented here—will help. My own young life in the loving care of my Polish nanny proved further testimony to deeds of individuals who surmounted their hostile times to save a Jew.

Yad Vashem, the Holocaust memorial and museum in Jerusalem, has honored more than 10,000 rescuers. (Our own Jewish Foundation for Christian Rescuers provides monthly stipends to 1,200 of them, 80 percent to Polish rescuers.) But because of insufficient evidence, we may never know about countless other episodes. We can only estimate the total number of rescuers (experts use a wide range, from 50,000 to 500,000). The stories Arnold Geier recounts in this volume suggest that the actual figure, though probably never more than one percent of Europe's population, could well be higher than current estimates.

Consider the stories presented in the pages that follow, about one family's laundress who hid Erich Segal on a nearby farm; about the German soldier who paid the author's grandfather a debt of gratitude by warning him of his scheduled arrest; about the Kiev resident who rescued Anna Lautman and about the woman on a farm outside Kiev who provided shelter for her. Consider the help extended to Benno and Jacob Elkus by the Van Tol family and by the Holzkorte family. Each story, skillfully constructed from interviews, tells us that Jews fleeing their predators frequently received unexpected assistance from their Christian friends and neighbors. This, I believe, is the power of this book. It suggests that uncharted escape routes were peopled not only by all-too-many bystanders and killers but also by an exceptional number of helpers.

What impressed me perhaps most about Mr. Geier's book is its unassuming style. In telling a stirring story, he allows its insights to speak for themselves. As a result, they strike us all the more poignantly. Stories, such as these, about rescuers are inherently moving. They don't need embellishment. We are grateful, then, to Mr. Geier for his self-restraint, for his skill in giving voice to forgotten heroes.

—ABRAHAM H. FOXMAN
National Director of the Anti-Defamation League of B'nai B'rith (ADL)

Under Doctor's Care

As told by Bianca Perlmutter Lerner

WARSAW, POLAND
MIAMI, FLORIDA

Our ticket on the mighty *Queen Mary* was for October 4, 1939. The Germans invaded Poland in September, so the *Queen* sailed without us.

We lived in a new residential area of Warsaw, in the first cooperative apartment building constructed in Poland. My father was a prosperous importer-exporter, with offices throughout Poland. He traveled extensively and spoke several languages fluently. My mother, a pediatrician, had an office near our home. They showered their love and attention on me, their only child, and sent me to a prestigious private school for girls even though I was the sole Jew among 500 other students. My best friend was Hanna, only child of Dr. Stanislav Popowski. We studied and played together, giggled and laughed as only ten-year-olds could, and spent much time at each other's homes.

In less than three weeks in September 1939, the Germans subdued Poland and conquered Warsaw, its capital. In October, all Jews were ordered to move into a walled area designated the Warsaw ghetto. Hanna's father, Dr. Popowski, offered to take me into his home until the "circumstances improved." Although my parents were considering the generous and daring offer, I would not hear of it. I wanted to be with my father and mother. So we moved into the ghetto with thousands of other Warsaw Jews.

Life was difficult but, at least for us, not impossible. My education never stopped. I was tutored in languages, history and mathematics by former teachers living in the ghetto. As a physician, my mother was treated with deference. She attended sick children and treated them as best she could. There were no medicines or surgical facilities, and the Germans had no interest in keeping Jews alive. She was required, however, to keep careful records and statistics of the diseases she encountered, and a tally of the deaths she witnessed.

Because of my father's reputation as a businessman and his flawless command of German, he was appointed director of the Umschlagplatz, the transfer point through which everything that entered or left the ghetto was recorded, checked, and routed for delivery. His office was next to a railroad siding which served as the arrival port of all ghetto supplies, and as the departure point of human cargo to the death camps throughout Poland. He reported directly to the German army colonel who was in charge of the transfer point, and, because members of the Wehrmacht (Regular Army) were not as murderous as those of the SS, he was also friendly with several of the Wehrmacht officers and soldiers who were guarding the perimeter of the ghetto.

One day in early April 1943, Mother was attending a sick child when she got caught in one of the periodic roundups conducted by the SS. She never re-

Dr. Stanislav Popowski

turned home from her visit of mercy. She was sent to Treblinka and disappeared. This tragedy convinced my father of the hopelessness of the situation and he decided to try and save me first, and then himself. He enlisted the aid of a trustworthy person in the Umschlagplatz to deliver an urgent message to our friend, Dr. Popowski, asking him to "take me under his wing." The doctor readily agreed and, a few days later, wearing my best clothes, I nonchalantly walked out of a ghetto exit where my father had bribed the German soldiers to look the other way.

Dr. Popowski met me at a prearranged corner, hugged me warmly, and took me home to his family. I was treated like one of their own. My friendship with Hanna blossomed into sisterhood. I remained with them for several months, but it was not a practical arrangement. All the family's friends and neighbors knew me and I had to hide in a closet every time anyone approached—leaving the house was out of the question. One evening, Dr. Popowski asked me to join him in his study after dinner. I obediently sat across from him while he relaxed in an easy chair. "Bianca, dear child," he began, "it is not good for you to live like this, hiding in a closet to avoid people and unable to enjoy a breath of fresh air. So we must do something about it. As you know, I am a lung specialist. My duties include taking care of the children in the Hoza Street Catholic Convent. I have made certain contacts and will be able to place you there among the orphans. But there are some important things you must remember, so listen carefully." I leaned forward in anticipation and with mixed emotions. On the one hand, it would be wonderful not to be confined, but, on the other, I dreaded leaving these wonderful people and facing a new environment alone.

Dr. Popowski continued, "In a few days, I will have new identity papers for you. Your name will be Janina Marzec, daughter of a carpenter and a peasant woman, both killed in the war. I will brief you about their history. Most of the orphans in the convent are from the lower economic class and your refined Polish doesn't blend in. I advise you to use more slang expressions and forget other languages altogether. You must not be conspicuous."

He then told me that only two people would know I was Jewish. One was the Mother Superior, Matka Matilda Getter, who apparently had hidden other children at risk of her own life. The other was her secretary, who was in charge of the convent in Matka Getter's absence. The Mother Superior supervised a large area surrounding Warsaw and often traveled from convent to convent. By taking her devoted secretary into her confidence, she could be sure that her Jewish charges were protected while she was away.

The following week, as dusk began to dim the daylight, Dr. Popowski brought me to the convent. I met the Mother Superior, and we took an immediate liking to each other. The doctor gave me a loving hug and promised to look in on me whenever he came to the convent.

Mother Superior sent me to a convent-owned farm in the country for two months to recover my strength. I ate well, picked flowers, and help feed the animals. When I returned, she made arrangements for me to be tutored in the city rather than sent to a public school where my identity might be revealed. I made rapid advances in my studies.

One day, when Mother Superior was away, all the girls were summoned to participate in confession. I had learned all of the Catholic prayers, but I didn't know what to confess. It was a major crisis in my young life. Then I remembered that everything having to do with sex was taboo, so when my turn came, I told the priest that I had thoughts about sex and boys. Apparently, I passed the test. The priest told me to recite Zdrowas Maryjo (Hail Mary) three times for absolution.

Matka Matilda Getter

Meanwhile, with his wife gone to an unknown fate and his child safely hidden, Father decided to leave the ghetto. He again bribed army guards and slipped out one night. Had he waited another day, escape would have been impossible. The ghetto uprising began on April 19, 1943, and the desperate Jewish resistance tied up the heavily armed Nazi forces. Eventually, the brutal SS troops systematically destroyed the ghetto house by house and slaughtered the 60,000 remaining Jews. There had been 500,000 the year before. By May 16th, the battle and the Jewish presence in the walled enclave was over.

Although my father had many Gentile friends, none was willing to hide him and, in fact, all were apprehensive about his sudden appearance at their homes. But one woman helped. Her mother visited her every day and left at dusk to return to her small apartment in one of the factory slum areas of Warsaw. She persuaded her mother to allow my father to stay with her in return for a weekly fee. In desperation, he accepted the arrangement and notified Dr. Popowski of his whereabouts.

A factory was directly across the street from the old woman's apartment, and someone peering from that direction could easily observe any movement near its windows. Therefore, Father had to be careful how and where he moved in the tiny room so that even his shadow could not be noticed. Everyone knew the old lady's routine, and any deviation might arouse suspicion. He lived there like a caged tiger for nearly a year. Twice during that time, I risked a visit with him. I would arrive in the evening when the woman was home, and would leave in the morning before she padlocked the door for her daily visit with her daughter. These reunions brought us closer together. We talked about my dear mother and dared not express her probable fate, and we gave each other courage to go on and to fight for survival.

When the Red Army approached the Vistula River in August 1944, the Poles of Warsaw rose in revolt against the Germans. There was an agreement between leaders of the Polish underground and Soviet authorities that, as soon as the uprising began, the Russians would shell the city to support the action and to force the Germans off the streets. But the Red Army guns were silent. The uprising was led by people loyal to the polish Government-In-Exile based in London, which the Russians opposed with their Soviet-controlled Polish government in Moscow. It was to their advantage to let the Germans and "unfriendly" Poles kill each other.

As soon as the fighting began, I told Mother Superior I wanted to join the underground. She blessed me and wished me good luck. The area around the convent was controlled by the Poles, and it was easy to find someone in authority and volunteer to help. I was given the code name Joanna, learned how to fire a pistol, and was designated a "runner." I would carry messages through connecting cellars of apartment buildings, through barricades, and over the rubble of demolished structures. They liked the little thirteen-year-old-Polish orphan girl and occasionally patted me affectionately on the head upon completion of a mission.

Unknown to me, my father had left the dingy apartment when the uprising started. He tried to make his way to the convent to see me before joining the Resistance. He had been an officer in the Polish Army and his experience could be useful. While darting across a street, a stray bullet caught him and lodged in his right lung. The underground fighters took him to a makeshift field clinic in an old school building. Because the wound was apparently not life-threatening and there were no facilities to remove the bullet, he remained unattended on a stretcher. When someone near him was treated and released, he persuaded the man to deliver an envelope addressed to me at the convent. When it arrived, Mother Superior gave it to an underground officer who passed it along to me. In it, my father wrote that he was hurt and told me where he was. Since I was supposed to be an orphan, he signed it "Your loving Grandma." I ventured to the field clinic between assignments. It tore me apart to see my father lying there, hungry for food and medical attention. Whenever possible, I visited him and brought him whatever I could pilfer. One time, I even brought him a clean sheet I had stolen.

After one month of fighting, the Resistance ran out of food, ammunition, and, with the Red Army still stagnating on the other side of the Vistula, the will to go on. The Nazis vowed to burn the city to the ground. The Poles decided to evacuate the field clinic to save the wounded. Father and I said our "good-byes" and consoled each other with a solemn promise to meet soon.

As I learned later, my dear father was finally given some attention. A Polish nurse who bathed him discovered he was circumcised and reported him to her superiors. An anti-Semitic Polish officer had him taken to a courtyard and executed. He had survived everything the Nazis devised to exterminate him, but he could not survive the hatred of his fellow officers and countrymen. He was only three months from liberation.

After the Germans overpowered the Resistance, they treated its participants as prisoners of war. The tide had turned against the Nazis, so they decided to gain favor and become more lenient. As the Red Army smashed westward, we were moved to eight different prison camps, sometimes on foot, other times by cattle car. Those who survived were finally delivered to the Bergen-Belsen death camp.

At one of the camps, we were housed near a fence, and on the other side were English and American prisoners of war. We could not speak to them, but were able to tie handwritten notes to small rocks and throw them over the fence when the guards were not in sight. Since I spoke several languages, including English, I became the translator for the barracks.

The messages were friendly (How long have you been here? Where do you live?), hopeful (Hang in there, it will be over soon), and even flirtatious (Are you blond or brunette? I would like to meet you when this is over). It added a tiny sparkle to our dreary lives. I included my background and mentioned that I had an uncle who had fled from Vienna to England. One English soldier responded and suggested that I write a letter on official POW mail and he would send this to his sister. Maybe she could locate my uncle. He was allowed to send monthly mail to England as I could to Poland. But I had no one and would not jeopardize Dr. Popowski or Mother Superior by writing to them. I followed the soldier's suggestion and, as I later learned, his sister somehow found my uncle and informed him that, as of the date of the letter, I was still alive.

A Polish tank division, fighting under General Eisenhower's command, liberated us from Bergen-Belsen in April 1945. I thought I would be better off as a Polish orphan, so I still told no one that I was Jewish.

From the Niederlangen Displaced Persons camp, I wrote letters to my uncle, and addressed these to him in various cities in England. Apparently, the Dead Letter Office of the British postal service noticed the many envelopes obviously searching for the same person. Incredibly, they inserted an ad in some of the popular newspapers, and my uncle was found. He wanted me to come to him, but the British would not issue a visa. In desperation, my uncle contacted a distant relative in the United States who found someone to prepare the affidavit required for immigration to America. In the Fall of 1945, the British finally granted me a temporary visa, and I lived with my uncle in Nottingham for a year, recuperating and adjusting to normal living. Then I sailed for America.

A few days after I joined my uncle, there was a knock on his front door. I sat near a window in the parlor reading a magazine but looked up as a young mild-mannered man greeted my uncle and asked to speak to him. My uncle invited him into the house, offered him a seat and looked at him expectantly. The young man sat on the forward edge of a couch, cleared his throat and began. He had been a prisoner of war in Germany and, at one camp, had been in contact with a young girl via "rock mail" and forwarded a letter in her behalf to his sister. Having just returned and

been discharged from the service, he obtained my
uncle's name and address and wanted to stop by to
find out what happened to the girl. My gasp and
shriek supplied him with the answer. It had never occurred to me we would meet someday. He stayed for
tea and light conversation and returned to anonymity.
I had forgotten to ask his name.

One of my first letters from England reached
Mother Superior, Matka Matilda Getter. She was delighted that I had survived, blessed me and hoped I
would keep in touch with her. We corresponded until

Bianca today

the early 1960s when one of my letters was returned, marked "Unable to deliver. Deceased."

I also wrote to Dr. Popowski to see if he and his family had survived. Although his home had been demolished during the fighting, the letter reached him. He responded immediately, amazed that I was still alive. They had all been taken to a labor camp, suffered from malnutrition and harsh treatment, but were liberated by the Russians. While searching for me, Dr. Popowski learned the details of my father's tragic death and passed it on to me as gently as he could. We continued our correspondence until he and his wife passed away.

Hanna Popowski, my childhood friend, became a professor of literature in a Polish university, married and raised a daughter who also became a college professor. Over the decades, we have exchanged memories, news and small gifts. But two years ago, Hanna sent me the greatest gift of all—her daughter, Agnieszka. She was a guest in my home during her visit to America and I tried to match the warmth, sincerity and hospitality her grandparents had shown me. Agnieszka was the image of her mother and even used the same hand gestures when describing something with enthusiasm. Her presence took me back to the past and when we parted. I was embracing her, her mother, the Popowskis, and my youth. I hope that she, at least, will return one day.

Lost and Found

As told by Fred Bachner

BERLIN, GERMANY
HARTSDALE, NEW YORK

We Bachners lived the life of most middle-class Berliners in the 1930s. Father operated a small business, manufacturing men's clothing, and Mother helped out whenever she was needed. My older brother James and I attended school like all other youngsters. To a 12-year-old like me, life was routine and pleasant.

Then came Kristallnacht, November 9, 1938. While uniformed Nazis and their sympathizers destroyed Jewish stores and set fire to synagogues, the Gestapo arrested Jewish males over the age of 13 for deportation or incarceration. They swept into our apartment and took my father and 16-year-old brother with them. They were immediately deported to Poland and went to Chrzanow, a small Jewish vil-

14

lage near Cracow, where my father was born and raised. In just a few days, my whole life seemed to have come apart. Father and James had always been there, and suddenly they were gone. I was devastated.

Mother immediately applied for the proper papers for us to leave Berlin and join Father and James in Poland. Finally, in June of 1939, we were able to board a train and were soon reunited in Chrzanow.

Although we realized that the political situation was unstable, we never dreamed that, only nine weeks later, like a spreading disease, the Germans would be back in our lives. They overran Poland, and even though we fled eastward for almost 35 miles, we were marched back to the village. We were trapped!

Everyone in Chrzanow was forced to work. Father and Mother worked in a factory making uniforms for the German Army. Early in 1940, James was taken to a labor camp in Upper Silesia. I tried deliberately to shut out the thought that I may never see him again. I was employed by a beverage distribution company. I would get up at 4 AM and clean the company's horses and stables, and later, with horse and wagon, deliver beer and sodas to German Army posts in the area, as well as to Aryan restaurants and canteens.

In early 1942, I was told to start delivering beer to the guards at a new labor camp, Trzebina, about 9 miles away. I followed orders and added the camp to my regular route. I was always outwardly cheerful and friendly with guards and was careful not to antagonize any of them. One day, I was chatting with one of the guards when, out of the corner of my eye, I spotted an inmate. He looked familiar. As I stared straight in his

direction, the inmate also looked up. I could not believe my eyes—there he was, my brother James! My
heart beat like a drum in my chest. Trying to appear
calm, I casually asked the guard if I might speak to my
brother for a few minutes. "Go ahead," he said. It was
wonderful to see him again and to find out what had
been happening to him. He had been worried about us
and was glad to hear we were alive and in relatively
good health. I couldn't wait to tell my parents!

I thought about James every night, how much I
missed him, and how I longed to find a way for my
parents to see him again. Then I had an idea. The next
time I made a delivery to Trzebina, I took along extra
items such as cigarettes and baked goods from the village and gave some to the guards. I sought out the
Sergeant of the Guards, delivered the usual order of
beer, added some of my cigarettes, baked goods, and
wine, and casually engaged him in conversation. I
asked him if the camp had facilities for the burial of inmates who had passed away during the week. As expected, he said there were no facilities. I then suggested
that I could come with my horse and wagon once a
week and take away the bodies in caskets and have
them buried in the village. Of course, I explained, I
would need an escort of 10 men to help wash the bodies and bury them in the Jewish tradition. The sergeant
told me to wait while he brought my proposal to the
camp commander. Much to my surprise, the commander agreed.

The following week, and for many weeks thereafter, I pulled into the labor camp with closed caskets
full of food and clothing for the inmates. In the area
where the bodies were stored, the prisoners emptied the

caskets and inserted the bodies. Then, under guard of three German soldiers, the wagon, followed by ten inmates, slowly covered the 9 miles to Chrzanow. At the local Jewish cemetery, the graves were dug and a brief memorial service was held. During the few hours of the temporary "freedom," the prisoners were fed by the townspeople, and new shoes and clothes were exchanged for the old. Even the guards were treated to a good meal. They knew that none of their charges would attempt to escape. After all, where could they go?

In this way, my parents and I were able to see our beloved James several times.

Then came Spring of 1943!

Poland was to be made Judenrein (clean of Jews). Very early one morning, I saw German soldiers sweep through the streets of the village. I thought they were looking for black marketeers. I ran from the stables to my mother to warn her to hide anything that was not "legal," but I was wrong. The soldiers took all adults, including my parents, to the central marketplace, marched them to the railroad station and onto waiting railroad cars. The train took them out of town, out of sight, and out of my life. I stood there alone, abandoned, and scared. I felt an emptiness I had never felt before.

I knew it would only be a matter of time before my turn came. I went to the local authorities and volunteered to be sent to Trzebina where my brother was. At least I would be with him and share whatever lay ahead. The cruel Germans accepted my offer and promptly sent me to a different labor camp. Now, my brother was gone too! My world had collapsed around me.

I survived heavy labor at three camps, worked in

a construction gang that converted a weaving plant
into a Krupp ammunition factory, and ended up in a
train to Auschwitz in the early summer of 1944. About
seven months later, with the cannons of the advancing
Red Army clearly audible, Auschwitz was disbanded
so that all evidence of the horrors could be obliterated.
For the inmates, the death march began.

Groups of hundreds walked westward through
the heavy snows. Those who fell or couldn't continue
were shot on the spot. At night, we stopped at a farm
and were ordered into a barn. I joined two fellows I
had been walking with. We collapsed into a heavy
sleep. The next morning, the two men told me they
could not go on and would stay in the barn when
the group reassembled. I warned them not to be
foolish. Surely, the Germans would burn the barn before they withdrew and both would perish. "What's
the difference," they said. They stayed. The Germans
didn't bother to burn the barn and just pushed on.
Both were rescued soon thereafter—seven months before me.

I walked almost 80 miles to Gross Rosen concentration camp, in Upper Silesia. There, inmates from
many other concentration and labor camps were
crowded into facilities that simply could not accommodate them. I was frantic. When I saw groups getting
onto a train transport, I pushed myself among them.
At that point, I didn't care where I would be going as
long as I could get out of Gross Rosen.

The train consisted of open cars, stuffed to capacity with emaciated prisoners. It was freezing, and snow
and rain fell continuously. There was no food other
than what heavenly liquid I could catch on my tongue.

As people died, we threw out their bodies to make room so the survivors could at least sit down. After two weeks, the few of us who were still alive arrived at our destination—Dachau!

I fell off the train, all skin and bones, barely able to move. But they wanted me for labor, so they permitted me to remain in the barracks and recover for two weeks. Then, one evening, they put me and about a dozen others into a truck and drove us to a satellite camp of Dachau, about 45 miles east, to help in the construction of an airplane factory near Muehldorf. We arrived well after dark.

It was a bitter cold night, and I could see inmates and guards huddled around small fires, trying to keep from freezing. As I waited beside the truck, I noticed a figure crouched near one of the fires. There was something familiar about him, I thought. I tried to attract the person's attention. I whistled, shouted, and waved my skinny arms. Finally, the figure turned, looked in my direction, shrugged, and inched toward me.

His face was hollow, the eyes deeply set in, the skin tight against bone. He came closer. I didn't dare express what I was thinking. Then I heard a whisper, so soft that I could barely make it out, and yet so powerful that I thought it would explode my eardrums. "Fredi, is that you?" "James?" We fell into each other's arms, tears streaming down our ashen faces, clinging to each other—all we had left of our past, our present, and our future.

James nursed me as best he could. He shared what little food there was to get me back to survivable strength, and we worked side by side. After about four months, the American Army was approaching the

Dachau area, and the Germans decided to take the inmates of our camp to the Alps for extermination. They wanted to leave no evidence of their crimes. Once again, I boarded a transport for an unknown destiny, but this time James was with me. We figured this would be our last ride together, our last ride ever.

As our train puffed its way toward Austria, there came a tremendous roar out of the sky. Dozens of American planes swooped low and began to strafe the transport. On top of each car were German soldiers with machine guns to guard us. At the sight of the planes, they jumped off the train to take cover. The engineer slowed the train down, probably to save himself, and James and I joined other prisoners who jumped off and disappeared into the fields adjoining the tracks.

We walked in the direction of the front line and, in the evening, came upon a farmhouse. James spoke fluent French and passed himself off as a French laborer and me as his deaf and dumb assistant. We thought we were free at last. But it was not to be. Within a few hours, the farmhouse was filled with German soldiers fleeing from the advancing Americans. We sneaked into a barn to spend the night. We didn't get much sleep because there was what seemed to be an unending barrage of artillery.

In the early morning hours, the guns were silent, and James and I crawled out of the barn. Daylight was just beginning to swallow the darkness. We came across dead soldiers, took their pistols, and made our way to the road. We noticed white flags in the windows of neighboring farmhouses, so we knew the Americans were not far away.

Suddenly, we were surrounded by an American patrol. We dropped our guns quickly and cried and laughed all at once. The combat soldiers must have wondered about the sanity of these two apparitions before them. They took us behind their lines to Headquarters.

At last, the odyssey of death and suffering was over. We told our story and were immediately released, treated, and transported to the rear.

After we recovered, we searched everywhere for our parents. We registered their names with Displaced Persons camps, and various organizations concerned with

Fred Bachner today

survivors. Eventually, we found our father in Berlin. He had been in several concentration and labor camps and had held on. Mother had been murdered in Auschwitz. So what was left of our little family was reunited.

In America, we began to rebuild our lives. Father remarried, and James and I married and raised our families. Although we eventually lived in separate areas of the country, the bond of our experience has kept us and will keep us tied together forever.

Kelev's Choice

As told by "Ester Milshtein"
(pseudonym for a survivor who
wishes to remain anonymous)

WARSAW, POLAND
JERUSALEM, ISRAEL

I was never afraid of people or dogs. When the Nazis entered my life, I became afraid of people. Before then, my family lived in a spacious apartment in Warsaw. My father, an electrical engineer, operated a successful small appliance factory. We had all the comforts of family life. Since I had no brothers or sisters, my father gave me a most loyal, loving, and obedient friend to keep me company while he and mother were at work.

He was a male terrier, with black eyes trustingly peeking through gray fur, and answering to "Motek." I played with him, teased him, bathed him and fed him.

24

Sometimes, after playing and rough-housing, Motek became excited and uncontrollable. I would talk to him, and my soft low voice seemed to get through and calm him. As a matter of fact, people used to say that my voice would quell an erupting volcano.

After the Germans came, we were forced to live in the Warsaw ghetto in very tight quarters, but Motek came with us. He was considered a member of the family.

Three years later, everything had changed. The Nazis murdered my father in the ghetto, my mother starved to death in a slave labor camp, Motek was shot by the Germans and the ghetto was burned to the ground.

I was transported to the infamous Majdanek death camp, near Lublin. Very few survived its gas chambers, which, as in Auschwitz, operated day and night. Soon after my arrival in the summer of 1943, I was unfortunate enough to be near a minor altercation among several prisoners. The tower guards fired into the group, and I was hit. A bullet passed through my right thigh.

At Majdanek, it was customary to kill sick and wounded inmates. The doctor who was called to the scene questioned me about the incident. I told him the facts and emphasized my innocent involvement. He thought for a moment and told me he would treat me at the clinic because he liked the sound of my voice.

I recovered just in time to be placed on the transfer list to the slave labor camp at Skarzynsko-Kamienna, also near Lublin, on the railway line to Treblinka. When I arrived, I was just 18 and, compared to others, was considered able-bodied for work. I was assigned the job of filling 20 mm. cartridge shells with explosives.

The Camp Kommandant was a tough SS officer who ruled with an iron fist. His men patrolled the area with vicious guard dogs to prevent resistance or escape. Living conditions were dreadful, food was scarce, facilities primitive, and hopeless despair dominated the prisoners. No one had a friend, except for me. Surprisingly, I shared him with the ruthless SS Kommandant.

I didn't know his name, but I called him Kelev, Hebrew for "dog." He was the only thing that seemed to bring an occasional smile to the hard face of the Kommandant. Kelev was a magnificent Great Dane, with smooth black and white fur contoured by every muscle into a picture of strength and power. His dark eyes were sad and penetrating. He had free run of the camp and sniffed and barked at the grimy prisoners. He frightened and terrorized them, but not me. I talked to him, petted him, played with him, and calmed him, and we became friends. The guards smiled tolerantly at the sight of the skinny girl communicating with the Kommandant's pet. They were more lenient and looked aside when I occasionally stood by as the dog was being fed. They may not have been so tolerant had they caught me helping myself to some of the dog food—it was a delicacy compared to what I had to eat. It meant so much to me to have someone to talk to, to care for, to caress, to be snuggled up against and to be slobbered over. It camouflaged my feeling of hopelessness.

One morning, after I had been in Skarzynsko-Kamienna about eleven months, we were ordered to assemble for "parade." I had survived several during the year. The prisoners were lined up and marched past a group of SS officers. The Kommandant stood in the background and observed the proceedings. Those who appeared healthy were motioned to one side to be shipped to factories which had requisitioned additional laborers, and those who looked too ill to work were ordered to the other side, to be shot.

By that time I had contracted typhoid, had lost my hair, and, at age 19, weighed less than 80 pounds. I was sent to join the condemned. Suddenly, I heard a yip and a bark. I looked up to see the Great Dane move away from the Kommandant, walk slowly, carefully, powerfully and majestically toward me, his eyes never leaving mine. His tail swung in a deliberate, even

A tender good-bye

beat like a metronome as he came alongside me to be caressed.

I bent over, smiled at him, talked to him, stroked his head and back, rubbed his sides, and softly said my farewell. He licked my bony hand. It would probably be the last act of affection I would ever receive—and that from a dog. Much to my surprise, the Kommandant suddenly called to one of the officers, motioned toward me, and I was ordered to leave the group of the dead and join that of the living. Kelev walked beside me, close to my bony legs, as I took my place among the lucky ones.

A few days later, I was transported to a munitions factory in the Buchenwald Concentration Camp complex near Leipzig. Ill as I was, I worked hard to survive. When the Red Army overran the area and liberated me nine months later, I was all skin and bones. But I was alive!

Today, I live in Israel, the only place in which I feel safe. It is not often that I think back to the horrible days of my youth. But sometimes when I sit on my balcony and watch children play or walk with their dogs, I remember Kelev. At first he represented companionship and hope. In the end, he represented life itself—my life.

The Exodus

As told by Kurt Weinbach

VIENNA, AUSTRIA
ROCHESTER, NEW YORK

It was a dark day for Israel (Izzy) Weinbach when the Serbian nationalist Gavrilo Princip assassinated Austrian Archduke Francis Ferdinand and his wife in Sarajevo. It was June 28, 1914, just a few days before Izzy's annual reserve duty in the Austrian Army was to end. The violent act of one deranged "patriot" immediately plunged the world into war, and Izzy remained in uniform until it was over four years later.

When his unit was sent to the Russian front, Israel Weinbach was a Corporal. Officially, he was a company clerk under command of Captain Heinrich Stumpfl. But his expertise with the primitive cameras of that era, which enabled him to take, develop, and print pictures in the field, caught his superior's attention. Officers of low rank never qualified for home

29

leave, so Captain Stumpfl and his aides unofficially
kept Corporal Weinbach busy taking personal pictures

Corporal Israel Weinbach in Russia during World War I

which they sent to their respective families. It was second best to being home.

Whenever photographic supplies were about to run out, Captain Stumpfl issued orders for Weinbach to travel to Vienna where Izzy not only stocked up on the supplies, but also bought liquor, sweets, and uniform parts (buttons, belts, insignia, etc.) for the Captain and his officers. Since his hometown near Lemberg (now known as Lvov in Russia) was on the train route to Vienna, he was able to visit with his family at least once each trip.

During the four years of living in close quarters, Israel Weinbach and Captain Heinrich Stumpfl became good friends, as good, at least, as was permitted between an officer and one of his men, especially a Jew. When the war ended, they parted with sincere wishes to one another, knowing they would probably never meet again.

Captain Stumpfl remained in the Army, served in various posts within Austria, and rose rapidly in rank. Israel Weinbach returned to his home which was now in Poland, married, and, when threatened with conscription into the new Polish Army, settled with his bride, Rose, in the beautiful and sophisticated Vienna he had learned to love over the years. There he opened a jewelry store and raised his two boys, Bert and Kurt.

Dark clouds gathered over Austria in the late 1930s. Strong Nazi elements clamored for a union with Hitler's Germany. In March 1938, encouraged by the timid actions of the Austrian government and the Western world, German troops marched into Vienna. They were greeted enthusiastically by the populace. Austria ceased to exist and became part of the Greater German Reich.

Soon thereafter, Israel Weinbach read in the papers that Austrian Brigadier General Heinrich Stumpfl had been promoted to Lieutenant General of the German Army, as well as civilian Stadtkommandant (City Commander) of Vienna, in charge of the capital city. Weinbach sent his old friend a short letter of congratulation. He considered it a matter of courtesy.

A few days later, a messenger delivered an invitation from the General for Weinbach to come to "an audience" at his headquarters, a former Habsburg palace. It was an offer one couldn't refuse. He took his 10-year-old son Kurt with him so the boy could inform his mother if Izzy were, for some reason, to be arrested or detained. Nothing was beyond consideration.

They were ushered into a huge waiting room which was decorated with large paintings of some of the former royal occupants, several sculptures, and uncomfortable-looking velvet-covered benches along the walls. On them, stiffly, quietly, and without the slightest hint of discomfort, sat military officers, police and Gestapo agents, and government and business men, waiting their turn to be received. Near the door to the "inner sanctum," a well-dressed middle-aged woman sat at a large desk, busily engaged in paperwork. In this atmosphere, Israel Weinbach presented himself and the letter of invitation, his boy hanging on to his sleeve with great apprehension. The secretary asked him to take a seat, rose with letter in hand, and disappeared through the door. She returned a few moments later and resumed her work.

Suddenly, the large doors opened and General Stumpfl appeared in its frame. He was tall, about 6'3", weighed about 230 pounds, and his bald head did not detract from his majestic appearance. He wore a dark green uniform, with silver-weave epaulettes and striking red lapels on his jacket, matching red stripes along the sides of his trousers leading to brightly-polished boots. The sight was awesome—certainly becoming an officer of general rank.

Everyone jumped to his feet and, as one, extended his right hand in the Hitler salute—except Izzy Weinbach and his boy. The general returned the salute with a sloppy wave of the hand, hesitated for a moment, looked at the people on his left, then on his right, spotted the pair and motioned them in.

Izzy was apprehensive, and Kurt was frightened. Once inside, General Stumpfl stood tall behind his desk and addressed his former corporal: "Weinbach, I ought to have you shot!" As he noticed the obvious panic in the eyes of his guests, Stumpfl smiled, extended his hand and remarked: "All these years, Izzy, we have lived in the same city and you never got in touch with me. Now, you finally remember that I exist. Thank you for your congratulations."

Father and son relaxed. The General and Izzy briefly exchanged pleasantries, brought each other up to date, and turned the conversation to the realities of the day. Stumpfl acknowledged that there may be "unpleasantness" in store for Jews, but he assured Izzy that he would help him, even at some risk to himself. With that, he shook hands with both of his visitors and ushered them through the door.

Within a few weeks, the unpleasantness began in earnest. Jews were harassed economically, politically, socially, and bodily. Everyone knew it would only get worse. Bert Weinbach, a young man almost 18, felt this keenly and made a decision. He would let no one dissuade him. He smuggled himself across the border to Czechoslovakia, but was caught and returned. He tried again, across the border to France, but with the same results. Finally, with another youth, he traveled through the Soviet Union with his German passport

German General Heinrich Stumpfl

prominently stamped with the letter J for Jude (Jew), and continued on to Tientsin, China, which was under Japanese occupation. He managed to get word of his safe arrival to his worried parents.

Izzy Weinbach also wanted to leave. Distant relatives in the United States were trying to arrange the proper papers for him, Rose and Kurt. Eventually, the American Consulate in Vienna issued a visa. After extensive efforts, Izzy found space on an Italian liner. It would leave Genoa on June 17th, 1940 and carry his little family to freedom.

But it was not to be. On June 10th, Italy joined the war as Germany's ally, and all sailings were cancelled. The Weinbachs were stuck in Vienna.

By the end of the year, Jews were forced to live in a specified district, and the elders of the Jewish community were given a quota of able-bodied persons to be delivered to the railroad station every Friday afternoon for "resettlement" in Poland. However, these elders also were given instructions not to include the Weinbach family in their Friday "delivery."

Izzy received a letter from Bert in China, assuring him of his well-being, and mentioning that other Jews had been able to come to China without papers. He enclosed an official-looking form from a Tientsin-based Jewish KUNST organization (a cultural club), assuring TO WHOM IT MAY CONCERN that the Weinbach Family would be accepted as members and entitled to all benefits such membership entails. Izzy didn't know what to do with such an "affidavit," and stashed it in a drawer.

On March 1st, 1941, the Vienna Inter-city Telegram Service delivered a sealed message to Israel Weinbach. It read: "Prepare to leave at once. Heinrich." Two days later, the head of the elders of the Jewish community called Izzy to his office and informed him that, for reasons unknown to him, the Gestapo had received direct orders from General Stumpfl to facilitate all arrangements necessary to send the Weinbach family out of Germany immediately. In which direction did Izzy plan to go?

Rose Weinbach, a very persuasive woman, decided to try an idea. She took the KUNST document from China to the Japanese Consulate. Pointing out that their German ally was arranging the journey and that the KUNST "affidavit" guaranteed they would not be a burden to the occupation authorities, she asked for a transit visa to Japan, permitting the family to continue from there to Shanghai and Tientsin, both under Japanese rule. To her great surprise and joy, the request was granted.

The Gestapo worked with typical German efficiency. They prepared visas, and made reservations with the Soviets on the Trans-Siberian Express for first class passage. Then, early one chilly March morning, Israel, Rose, and Kurt Weinbach, luggage in hand, left Vienna's North Railroad Station—probably one of the last legal exits of Jews from Germany.

General Heinrich Stumpfl of the German Army survived the war and was brought before the Allied De-Nazification Board in Vienna. They declared him innocent of any war crimes and attested that he had been an anti-Nazi, indirectly involved in the July 1944 plot to kill Adolf Hitler. The general died in 1972.

The Weinbach family survived in China and remained there until six months after Mao's communist armies overran their area. They left on a ship chartered by the American Joint Distribution Committee for Hong Kong and on to Israel. Izzy died there only two months later. The others remained in the new state for

Kurt Weinbach today

eight more years, and eventually joined other relatives in the United States.

It was a journey that started in 1914 in Austria-Hungary, a country that no longer is, and ended 35 years later in Israel, a country that, until then, never was.

Instant Adulthood

As told by Abe Argasinski, formerly Erich Segal

Lvov, Poland
Miami Beach, Florida

As a 12-year-old boy, just two weeks away from my Bar Mitzvah, I was neither aware of nor, frankly, gave much thought to the events which were overcoming my family, my country, or, as it turned out, human history. My life in Lvov, Poland, was pleasant enough and centered around school, Mother, Father, my younger brother Ernest and my pigeons.

I had eight pigeons in a coop on the roof and cared for them lovingly. I had eleven more in the attic of a little house near my father's lumberyard, about nine miles from Lvov. The yard sat between two forests, with adjoining villages, one inhabited by Poles, the other by Ukrainians.

The Poles and Ukrainians did not get along, and

every few months they would clash. When the Poles celebrated a religious holiday and didn't work, the Ukrainians went into the "Polish" woods and cut timber which they brought to my father to buy. The Poles would ambush the intruders with knives and sticks, and blood would flow. During a Ukrainian holiday, the situation reversed, and Polish blood was shed.

Since my father's mill operated day and night, he lived in the small three-room house during the week. Members of the family would come whenever possible and stay with him. He knew of my love for pigeons and had the attic divided into two sections—one as a laundry room, and the other, with a window opening onto the roof, as a pigeon coop. He also built a secret compartment into the floor of the first section to hide some jewelry and cash for an emergency.

During the first week of September 1941, there was a Christian holiday and, as usual, we were going to the lumberyard to spend a few days with Father. Too impatient to wait for my mother and brother, I took a trolley to the last station and made my way to the yard, walking and getting rides from farmers who knew me. I arrived there at mid-morning. After a short visit with Father, I went to the house, climbed the narrow stairs to the attic and tended to my pigeons. I was thrilled to see one of them sitting on several eggs. I had never seen pigeons being born. When I counted the flock, there was one missing. I climbed out the window onto the roof to see if it was there—it was. Down below, I saw Father greeting Mother and Ernest as they arrived at the yard.

About 20 minutes later, Mother called to me from downstairs that lunch was ready. "I'll be there in a minute!" I responded and turned my attention back to my pigeons. She called again and again, and each time I assured her I would come right down. Finally, I decided I'd better do as I was told. Mother would punish me with the snap of a towel to show her displeasure, and I wanted to avoid that. Suddenly, I heard loud sounds, like gunfire. The pigeons panicked and, with a fluttering noise, flew off, all except one. She remained on her eggs to complete her destiny. There was more shooting and I became very frightened. I went into the laundry room and hid under a big wash tub by turning it over me on the floor. The rat-tat-tat of gunfire continued and I trembled. I must have lost consciousness in my panic. When I awoke, all was quiet.

Boy, am I going to get it now, I thought. Mother will really let me have it with the towel for not coming down in all this time. Gingerly, I climbed down the steep stairs toward the kitchen.

The sight which greeted me is to this day engraved in my mind. Father, Mother and Ernest lay in pools of their own blood, their bodies riddled with bullets from Ukrainian rifles. They stared into nothingness. I screamed with all my might. "Mama, Mama." The echoes of my anguish bounced off the walls and the sound made me even more frantic. In a matter of minutes, my life had been transformed into a nightmare. When my voice gave out, I sat for a few minutes on the stairs and had only one desire—to get away from there fast.

I remembered the hiding place in the attic and emptied it of jewelry and about 3,000 Zlotys, a lot of money. I stuffed it in my pockets and ran to the home of a woman who was our family laundress for as long as I could remember, and whose husband worked in the lumberyard. When she asked about my parents, I blurted out the details of our tragedy. "What should I do?" I cried. She gave me a pair of shoes and a few clothes, put a large cross on a chain around my neck and said: "Don't tell anyone you are a Jew. Come with me. I will take you to my sister." We walked through the woods for about 8 miles and arrived at an isolated farm house. On the way, I gave the washerwoman 500 Zlotys for the shoes and clothes. She didn't want to take the money but I insisted. She advised me to hold on to what was left. I would need it in the future.

The sister remembered me as an infant and greeted me warmly. She assured me that she had room for me, that I would eat well and she would take care of me. I would join her daughters, both a few years older, and help with the care of several cows and lambs in the fields. The washerwoman gave me a warm hug and kiss and left.

The following day, I walked to the meadows and found the girls near a campfire with other young people whose animals were grazing nearby. Apparently, the girls had let it slip that a Jew was living with them. Someone shouted, "Jewboy, Jewboy!" I vehemently denied it and, at the first opportunity, rounded up the animals and returned to the house. Next morning, while everyone was in church, I gathered my few belongings and left for the woods.

At the other end of the forest was Rudaldanietska, a large and rich village. Just as I passed the majestic church in the village square, worshippers came out the doors and congregated in small groups in the area. I greeted everyone with the customary "Praised be Jesus Christ." They returned my greeting with a smile and a wave. When I approached a group of about twenty men discussing politics, I greeted them with "Praised be Jesus Christ," and added "I am looking for work. I can take care of animals." One of the men immediately replied that he could use help on his farm. Another was more persuasive. "Not only do I have a few animals that need attention, but I am a blacksmith and I will teach you the trade. It will be good for you in the future." That made sense to me and I accepted.

My new employer was Kazi Witkowski, a widower with one son who lived with his family at the other end of the village. He took me to his house, pointing out his grazing lands on the way, and led me into a small but comfortable room. "I forgot to ask, young man," he remarked, "what is your name?" I was unprepared for that. The name Erich Segal would immediately brand me a Jew, no matter how large the cross around my neck. At that moment, I remembered that I had planned to express my condolences to my Polish school teacher, Mr. Argasinski, at the accidental drowning of Leszek, his son and my school buddy. "Leszek Argasinski," I replied.

Mr. Witkowski treated me like a father would. He taught me his trade, which I eagerly learned. I had talent in my hands. On Sunday, when he went to another village to visit his sister and her ailing husband, I made my way to the village where Mr. Argasinski lived. Father and I had often visited him there. He was warm and friendly and had heard of my family's fate. I expressed my sorrow at the loss of his son. He wept. "Professor," I pleaded, "I am without papers. Please let me have Leszek's documents." Without hesitation, the sad-faced man gave me his son's identity papers, which were more valuable than gold. With these, I could prove that I was Leszek Argasinski. I quickly walked back to my village before anyone knew I had gone.

About four months later, I was working in the shop with Mr. Witkowski when a husky young man of about 30 entered. He greeted my boss and came toward me. "So, there's the boy you told me about!" he exclaimed. My heart stood still for a moment. What did he mean by that? Mr. Witkowski smiled and introduced Mr. Kalju, commander of the local partisans. "Come with me," Kalju suggested in strong tones of command, "You will meet the others." I followed him to the general store in the village square where just about everything anyone could need was sold. Toward the rear, there was an entrance to a cellar. We went down into a huge storage room containing supplies of all sorts. There were about 400 men sitting around. The conversations stopped when we appeared, and Mr. Kalju announced, "Men, this is our newest associate, Leszek Argasinski." They greeted me warmly and they made me feel comfortable.

I was assigned to a squad of 12 men. We received training in shooting, use of hand grenades and handling explosives. I turned out to be an excellent marksman. We worked during the day, and, at night, units would be sent 30 to 50 miles away to blow up bridges or roads. The Germans concentrated their garrisons in the larger cities and stayed out of the small villages.

Railroad workers would inform the partisans of military trains scheduled to come through the area, their destination, and, sometimes, the contents of their cars. Partisan units would tear up the rails, destroy bridges, or ambush the train and, when possible, capture the valuable military supplies destined for the front. As a result, the partisans always had plenty of guns and ammunition.

Because I was an outstanding shot, I was assigned special missions of assassination. These included several SS and Gestapo agents, two SS women officers, and a traitorous teacher. Once, I was ordered to kill the SS Kommandant of a nearby village area. We knew he left his office every night at precisely midnight. My two teammates and I hid behind some bushes directly in front of the entrance door. It began to drizzle. At exactly 12 o'clock, the door opened, bathing the immediate area in bright light. I held my breath as the Kommandant's dog jumped down the few stairs, barking and yelping at us behind the bushes. They forgot to mention the dog, I thought. Would he give us away? The Kommandant gave a harsh command: "Komm, Putzi, komm!" And like a good German, the dog instantly obeyed. He whined a little as he returned to his master's side. There was a triumphant smile on the SS officer's face as I aimed, squeezed the trigger twice in rapid succession and the bullets partitioned his head into unrecognizable fragments. The rest of him fell with a thud, and we ran into the night, leaving a whining dog standing over his master.

Two days later, the Nazis hung 58 Poles in retaliation.

I lived with Mr. Witkowski almost four years, and most of the time, he left me alone in the shop, confident that I knew the work and did it well. He was often away for a few days at a time, visiting with his sister, whose husband had finally died. Meanwhile, I tended to the cows, pigs and chickens, took care of customers, and helped older people who needed a strong arm to perform some chore they couldn't handle. I was swamped with work. The Germans were bogged down on the Russian front and devoted little of their attention or forces to small villages like ours. We rarely saw them, except when we ambushed them at night some distance away.

One day, Mr. Witkowski's son stopped by. I had seen him once before and had exchanged greetings. He talked to me as to a servant. "Did you cut enough hay for tomorrow morning's feeding?" he demanded. "Not yet," I replied, "I have been too busy." With that, he slapped me hard across the face and ordered: "Well, get to it, now!" I seethed with anger. The image of my family lying in pools of blood dominated my mind at that moment and I wanted to kill him right then and there. But I controlled myself.

Someone had a radio and told us that the Russians were approaching. In fact, I could hear the dim sounds of battle coming closer. I made my decision, took some food, clothing, ammunition, and my rifle and went into the forest, heading toward the front lines to find the Russians. I walked from village to village. In some, the Germans were still reported in the area, and in others they had fled. While walking through a wooded area, I heard a rustle in the trees above, and before I could look up, two Russian soldiers fell on me, pinned me down and disarmed me.

"You are a spy," they screamed at me. "No, no," I screamed back, "I am a Jew!" They took me back to their encampment and turned me over to an officer. "So you are a spy," he began again. "No, no, no, I am a Jew. Can't you understand? I am a Jew," I insisted. "We'll see, spy," the officer said. He looked around until he spotted another officer, obviously of high rank, with several medals displayed on his chest, including the Order of the Red Star, one of the highest awards for bravery. He called the officer over. "Colonel Wilenski," he said, "this man claims to be a

Jew." The officer studied me closely. I certainly didn't look Jewish, and the large cross resting on my chest was hardly supportive of my claim. Then he spoke. "Say the blessing over bread." I began: "Baruch attah adonai, eloheynu melech haolom . . ." He broke into a grin, embraced me with an authentic Russian bear hug, and kissed me on both cheeks. After I told him about my parents and my activities with the partisans, he assured me that I would never again have to worry about anything. "I am the commander of this unit, and you will stay with us." I was issued a new uniform, a Russian weapon, and, at 16, was considered one of the men.

Our unit fought its way toward Berlin, taking few prisoners. It was bloody and tough. I had had enough. I approached my friend and commander, Colonel Wilenski, and asked him to give me papers which would allow me to go back to Lvov and see if I could find anyone there who survived. He granted me that wish and, with a warm embrace, we parted. I commandeered a car from a German and drove east. Whenever I was stopped, the Colonel's papers were enough to let me proceed.

I never returned to Lvov. When I reached Breslau, I discovered that a Zionist group had formed a Kibbutz to train Jewish survivors for life in Palestine. Many were young people like me, and I felt comfortable with them. I worked as a blacksmith and handyman, married one of the survivors, raised a family, and lived in Breslau for over twenty years. By the mid-1960s, almost every Jew had left the

Abe Argasinski today

area, and we who had remained went to Israel to join the others.

It's been a hard and brutal existence for me. I have many regrets, but the greatest of them is that I lost my family and with it my childhood.

I wonder to this day how it feels to be a teenager.

The Kidnapping

As told by Jean Janina Hirsch Schechter

BUKACZOWCE, POLAND
MARGATE, FLORIDA

For me, the only good that came of the Russian occupation of our part of Poland was that I met Philip. We worked together in an office for the Soviet authorities, fell in love and married in 1940. We were lucky to find an apartment in Bukaczowce, a small village southwest of Cracow. We knew that Jews had never been accepted in this community so, in order to avert suspicion, we lived as Christians and went to church every Sunday.

A few months earlier, my husband had found someone who, for a price, could produce official-looking Polish identification papers, and we became Frank and Janina Rogalski.

The Germans arrived in June 1941, and our

daughter Barbara was born in September. We kept a low profile. Mostly, we were concerned about the teenagers who could spot a Jew a mile away, like a hunting dog can sniff its quarry. Philip began to tutor small children in various elementary school subjects

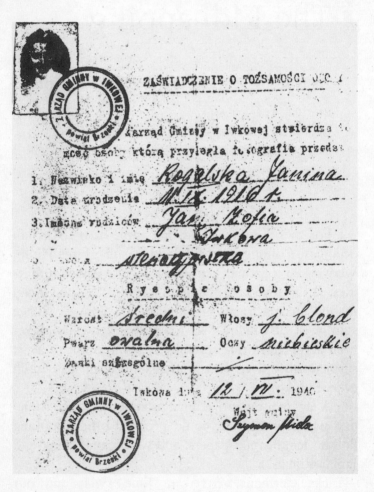

Forged Polish I.D. of Janina Rogalski

and was paid with bread, vegetables, meats, cloth, and other useful items that were not obtainable for money. It kept us alive. Fortunately, the younger children didn't suspect their teacher was Jewish.

We heard about the terrible things happening to Jews in the surrounding towns and villages. At first, the Nazis assembled the Jews, gave them shovels to dig their own graves, and filled them as fast as they were dug. Then, the Nazis ordered all Jews in the villages to move to a ghetto in Rohatyn, about 170 miles west of Cracow. There, the killings could be conducted with greater efficiency. We ignored the order and remained in our village. We had nothing to lose and life itself to gain.

One day, I went into the village center to find some milk for Barbara. A group of teenagers spotted me. One pointed and, grabbing his buddy's shoulder, shouted, "Look, Staschu, there's a Jew!" I cursed and threatened them for insulting me. They backed off. But I was quivering inside. It would only be a matter of time before we were discovered.

One Sunday in the summer of 1942, our landlord, Mr. Marcinkowski, came to us after we returned from church. Hat in hand, eyes toward the floor, he said in quiet tones, "I know that you are Jews and I have not told anyone, not even my wife. But you must leave now because I can't risk my family's life anymore. I promise I will not give you away. Good luck." With that he left.

Philip and I talked all night and decided to separate. I didn't look particularly Jewish, and we felt that, with me, the baby would have the best chance to survive. Philip, on the other hand, had certain Jewish features. Alone, he could probably hide in the woods or find work on the farms in the country. I told my husband that I would kill the baby and myself if we were caught. Some wealthy Jews bought cyanide for that purpose, but I could only afford a razor blade.

The next morning, after a tearful and emotional farewell, Philip walked northward and disappeared over a hill. Would our baby ever see her father again?

The Germans were critically short of farm labor and were always recruiting women workers for the fields. I packed a small suitcase, took my baby and false papers to the church and awaited the arrival of the German truck that picked up the volunteers. They drove to several farms, dropping women off at each. Finally, in the afternoon, we arrived at our destination. We stayed in a storage room in the farmer's house.

Every morning, I took my baby with me into the fields. While I worked, little Barbara would lie on a pillow in the shade of a shed or bush, frequently demanding attention as all babies do. The feeding, diaper changing, and general baby care interfered with my work. After a week or two, the farmer sent me to another farm. The same happened there. I worked that way for several months, and was fired from six jobs. The last farmer advised me to go back to Poland with my daughter. I had no choice. We would have to accept whatever awaited us there.

A farmhand drove us by horse and wagon to Durnholz, near Vienna, the nearest village that had a bus stop. While I sat in a makeshift waiting area for the bus, a tall, thin woman approached. "Are you Janina Rogalski?" she asked.

My look of surprise and bewilderment gave her

the answer. "Don't be frightened," she continued, "I was given your name by Herr Landesmann, the farmer who had to send you away. He told me about the problem with the little girl." I visibly relaxed. She continued, "I am Frau Birne and I own the inn here in town. I need someone to clean the rooms, help in the restaurant, and serve my guests. You will have a place to sleep, plenty of food, and some spending money. But you can't bring the baby with you. We have a very fine lady, a good Christian woman, who has a beautiful home and wants to raise a child. She will take good care of her. But there is one condition. You can visit the child once in a while, but not as her mother. We don't want to make trouble for the little girl or the woman who will give her everything she needs. Do you agree? Do you want to come with me?" I hesitated, but not for long. We would both be safe for the time being.

Most of Frau Birne's guests were men from Vienna who came for a few days of relaxation. Among them were military officers and Gestapo agents. Frau Birne, a pretty and shapely woman, was expert at providing diversion and recreation. Her husband was somewhere at the Russian front and she missed his lovemaking. Some of her guests eagerly made up for her loss, and they even brought her presents. She certainly was never lonely.

Several months after I began working at the inn, I was given the opportunity to visit the woman who had my child. She lived in the country, about a half-hour bus ride to the east. Her name was Berta Antelman, and she was a single woman in her mid-40s, full-bodied, with gentle blue eyes. She was deeply religious and went to church every day, taking Barbara with her. She showed me the beautiful clothes she had made for my little girl, and assured me the child was healthy and happy. Then she called my daughter in from the garden. Barbara toddled in playfully, followed by a small dog with a loud yelp. Her puffy cheeks and rounded face were proof that she was obviously well fed and cared for. It made me very happy momentarily until I realized that she did not recognize me. "Ja, Mutti?" she asked Berta Antelman. I was introduced as a nice lady who comes from the village from time to time and brings eggs and fruit. I had to be satisfied with this and hide the terrible anguish that gripped me. At least I could see my baby once in a while.

On my next visit a few weeks later, Fraulein Antelman took me into a room and opened the door to a closet in which there was a collection of elegant and expensive clothes, jewel boxes with precious stones, antiques of obvious value, and other items. She confided that they belonged to several Jewish neighbors who had to leave. She was holding them for their return. This gave me a feeling of confidence that Berta Antelman was the right person to take care of my Barbara.

The work at the inn was overwhelming. I cleaned the rooms, removed the ashes from the stoves, prepared food for the pigs and washed and ironed for the inn as well as for the guests. I also had to be at Frau Birne's beck and call day and night. But I was willing to endure anything as long as I could occasionally visit my baby.

Frau Birne gave me permission to see Barbara the following Monday. I stayed up until 3 AM the previous night to complete whatever chores needed to be done so there could be no complaints due to my absence. The following morning, ready to leave, I wanted to extend the courtesy of a "goodbye" to Frau Birne.

Berta Antelman

The door to her office was slightly ajar, and as I opened it, I caught her on the lap of an officer. She quickly jumped off and looked embarrassed. "I'm sorry," I stammered, "I just wanted to let you know I am leaving." She yelled, "No, you are not! Go back to your work!" "But, but, Frau Birne . . . ," I began. Her finger pointed to the door. "Go," she ordered, "get back to work."

I was furious. The anticipated visit was my personal holiday and I was looking forward to it with such longing. I thought about it as I completed the remaining chores, with bitterness in my heart. The following morning, I did not feed the pigs but sneaked out of the house, caught the bus and visited Barbara. An hour later, Frau Birne appeared at the Antelman house, in a rage. "You ungrateful little bitch," she shouted. "If you don't come back to the inn right now, I will denounce you to the Gestapo!" I don't know where I got the courage, but I replied in firm tones, "If you report me to the Gestapo, I will tell your best friend, Frau Munster, that you are seducing her husband." There was a tense moment that ended in a complete change in Frau Birne. She admitted "she was only joking," waited for me to conclude my visit, brought me back to the inn and gave me clothes, shoes and even a hat.

There were strong rumors that the war was coming to an end. There was much movement and migration of Polish workers toward the oncoming Red Army from the east, and others were moving toward the Americans in the west. I had mentioned this to Fraulein Antelman during my last visit and casually wondered out loud if that would make it possible to regain my child. She was adamant and reemphasized that the little girl was now hers and would remain with her. I dropped the issue and talked about other things. But I had a plan.

During the second week of April 1945, I made what ostensibly was to be my last visit to Fraulein Antelman. I told her I planned to return to Poland the following week. The Russians were rapidly approaching the area, and she understood my desire to return to my own country. I came, as always, with a few gifts for Barbara and some delicacies for her. When Fraulein Antelman began a household chore, I casually suggested that I take Barbara for a walk. She agreed. So we slowly strolled through the garden and toward the meadow beyond.

As soon as we were completely out of sight of the house, I picked my child up and ran toward the road visible on the horizon. The child became frightened at my sudden moves and screamed for her "Mutti." But for me it was now or never. As I continued to run, the sound of an airplane came toward us. It was a single American bomber, flying low overhead. I threw myself on the ground, covering my little treasure with my body. For a moment I thought how ironic it would be to make it this far and then be killed by an American bomb. But the plane flew on.

The road was crowded with refugees walking or riding their horses and wagons in either direction. We joined those heading west. Before long, someone in a wagon noticed me, carrying a small child, and offered us a lift. He was headed for Stuttgart, which had been captured by the French and Americans. As the days dragged on, our column was often passed by German vehicles filled with officers who were fleeing the advancing Russians and who wanted to surrender to the more lenient Americans. We got to Stuttgart eight days later.

What a joy it was to see American soldiers. They were kind to refugees, smiled at the children, treated them to sweets and directed the adults to the Displaced Persons camp established for survivors.

In the camp, I registered under the name Rogalski and was assigned a room in a house filled with other refugees. Although Barbara and I were in rags, I was happy that we could stop running. Down the street, the American Joint Distribution Committee had assembled a food kitchen where we could obtain hot nourishing meals.

One afternoon about a week after we arrived, there was a soft but firm knock on our door. I shouted, "Come in, the door is open."

When the figured entered, all I could see were the highly polished black boots, the kind worn by the

Jean and Barbara in Germany

Gestapo, and my fear instinct instantly overwhelmed me. This was heightened as my eyes traveled upwards and saw the leather coat loosely covering the man's well-built torso. Then I saw his face! With a triumphant smile, there stood Philip, my beloved husband. I almost fainted from surprise and joy. We fell into each other's arms and wept shamelessly. Little Barbara looked puzzled. Philip lifted his 4-year-old daughter up to his chest and smothered her with kisses. He had not held her since she was an infant. His warmth and sincerity got through to the child. She responded and seemed to understand that this was the Daddy I had told her about and who loved her.

After we exhausted our emotions and relaxed, Philip told me how he had managed to survive. He had gone deep into the farm areas and, as Frank Rogalski, worked as a helper. The German occupation authorities left the farmers alone as long as they delivered the expected production. He kept a low profile and remained in Saxony until the war ended. Then he registered under both his real and assumed name at the same Displaced Persons camp in Stuttgart and returned to Saxony. After I had registered, a clerk remembered the name Rogalski and contacted him, asking if he were related to a Janina and daughter Barbara. Philip was overjoyed but wanted to surprise us. He swapped what he could to obtain the leather coat and boots from a German. Philip wanted to look his best when he reentered our lives.

We briefly returned to Poland to search for any family survivors. Philip found four of his sisters, but I found no one. With the help of the American Joint

Distribution Committee and an aunt in New York, we sailed to America. The Statue of Liberty seemed to smile at us as we slowly entered the harbor, and we

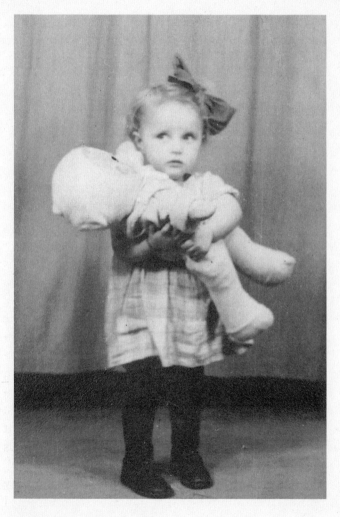

Barbara greeting her father

smiled back. She was the most beautiful sight I had ever seen. Indeed, we were the tired, the poor, the huddled masses yearning to breathe free. By the light of her raised torch, we began a new life.

Broken Glass, Broken Lives

By Arnold Geier

BERLIN, GERMANY
MIAMI, FLORIDA

It was the spring of 1915. The battle was ferocious. One German soldier, preparing to sprint ahead, suddenly caught a bullet, screamed, and fell. About twenty yards behind him, another soldier crawled along the ground until he reached the wounded one, and slowly dragged him by the belt toward a trench at the rear. Medics were waiting with a canvas stretcher and carried the bleeding soldier away.

In wartime, this was not an unusual incident, and it was soon forgotten.

For Jews in Germany, 1938 was not a good year. Special laws, specifically aimed against them, had been passed in the last two years, limiting the social, political, and economic activities of their daily lives. The handwriting was on the wall, but not all Jews saw it clearly. Although some had left as soon as Hitler had come to power, others were convinced that the political winds would change and that persecution belonged to bygone days and would never be revived by a civilized nation in the 20th Century. Many had made contacts with relatives, friends, and organizations hoping to find someone to sponsor them for emigration to a specific country or to any country that would have them. So it was not unusual to hear of a Jew in Germany who was planning to emigrate to the U.S., Shanghai, Colombia, Cuba, England, Palestine, or South Africa. But most Jews had no friends or relatives abroad and simply faced their uncertain future with trepidation mixed with hope.

My family was lucky. Mama's sister and her husband had moved to New York in the 1920s, in search for the "good life." My uncle worked as a night-janitor in a skyscraper. The family lived in a low-rent state-supported apartment project in Brooklyn. They had no money, but they had compassion, love, and courage. My aunt set out to help us by finding someone wealthy enough to qualify as a sponsor, as required by law. She called and searched all over New York. She pleaded, cajoled, and begged every prospect until she found one, an orthodox Jewish brassiere manufacturer, who was willing to sponsor our family and my grandparents and aunt for immigration to the U.S. This was no small task. It meant preparation of an "affidavit" consisting of disclosure of financial holdings, copies of tax returns, and a sworn guarantee that the sponsor would support the newcomers so they would not become a financial burden to the U.S. government.

In the fall of 1938, we received our affidavit on a

Thursday, and Papa immediately brought it to the U.S. Embassy in Berlin to register it and to receive a number. My grandfather decided to hold his over the weekend and to have an attorney-friend verify that all was in order. When he brought it to the Embassy on Monday morning, the quota had closed. His affidavit was not accepted.

In a "Jewish area" of Berlin, Grandpa, Grandma, and Aunt Dora were in their apartment on the evening of November 8th, when they heard a firm knock on their door. Grandpa froze. In Germany, such knocks usually meant trouble. The knock sounded again. With fear and apprehension in his heart, Grandpa opened the door slightly. There stood a tall man with strong Germanic features, dressed in a gray suit. He seemed to crowd the door, casting furtive glances to each side, as if he did not want to be seen there. "May I come in, please." It was not a question but a command. Grandpa stepped back and the man quickly entered, closing the door behind him. He remained standing as if frozen to the spot. "Herr Geier, I can only stay a minute." Grandpa held his breath. The man looked down, avoiding Grandpa's eyes. "Herr Geier, do you remember when you saved a soldier on the battlefield many years ago? I am that soldier." Like flood waters bursting a dam, almost forgotten memories overwhelmed Grandpa. At first, he had put the incident on the backshelf of his mind. After the Nazis came to power, he had forced himself to forget it altogether. "I work with the Chief of Police in Berlin and have kept track of you for a long time. Listen carefully now. Tomorrow night, police and SS will round up adult male Jews all over Germany. I have seen the list, and your name is on it. Do whatever you wish." He paused. Now his eyes met Grandpa's. "My debt to you is paid. Auf Wiedersehen!" And with that he turned, went through the door and disappeared into the darkness.

Grandpa was stunned. It took him several minutes to realize what had just happened. He trembled with fear and bewilderment, then quickly called my father and told him to come right over. He did not dare to say anything on the phone, so Papa was very concerned and took a taxi. Grandpa told him what happened, and both men knew they had to do something and quickly. After deliberating, they arrived at a plan. For the rest of that night and most of the following day, Grandpa and Papa were on their telephones spreading the news of the arrival in town that evening of Mr. Malach Hamoves (Hebrew for the angel of death). They suggested that he be greeted by all of our friends and their friends, and that news of his arrival be passed along to other interested parties. Those who were called presumably were warning their relatives and friends. Hundreds were probably contacted during those 12 hours. In late afternoon, Papa told us that he was going on a business trip for a while, kissed Mama, and left. To a 15-year-old girl and her 12-year-old brother, this didn't appear unusual. Actually, he took public transportation to the home of one of his customers, a self-professed anti-Nazi, who had offered to shelter him for a few days. So Papa spent the night there—to him it was the night of November 9th, 1938, and to history it would become Kristallnacht.

Early the next morning, I was suddenly shaken out of my sleep by a large hand on my shoulder. The shock forced my sleepy eyes open. There above me was a man. He looked like a giant, in a black uniform with silver emblems and decorations. He shouted: "Where is your father!" I was never so scared in my life. The words barely left my lips. "He's on a business trip some-where." The giant let go of my shoulder. He looked under my bed, in the closet, grumbled, and left to search the other areas of the apartment. When he found noth-ing, he confronted Mama with anger. I could hear her promise him, in a soft and pleasant voice, that she would have Papa call him as soon as he returned. Fi-nally, the Nazi left. Mama quickly tried to calm us and assured us that everything would be all right. She rushed us to get dressed and have some breakfast.

While we were eating, the noise level from the street below seemed to swell. Suddenly, there were sounds of breaking glass, and a mixture of shouts, or-ders, and laughter, blending with screams of terror. We rushed to the window, three stories above the street, and saw hundreds of men, women, and children milling about, watching groups of storm-troopers in action. One was smashing the windows of nearby shops, destroying their displays, and painting their walls with Stars of David and anti-semitic slogans. DIE JEW! DON'T BUY FROM JEWS! THE JEWS ARE OUR MISFORTUNE! Another group was beat-ing a bearded elderly Jew with nightsticks and bare fists. When I saw the blood streaming from the old man's face as his beard was being pulled off, I went wild. "No, no, leave him alone!" I screamed out the window in my 12-year-old voice. Of course, my plea was promptly lost in the tumult below. The police stood nearby and watched. No one interfered. Mama pulled me away from the window, held me and my sis-ter close to her bosom, and I cried like I had never cried before. Where was Papa? I wondered.

My father had spent the night with his German customer, hoping that Grandpa's alarm was a false one. By early morning, the radio news reports of a "spontaneous citizens' outburst" against Jews all over the city and throughout the country convinced Papa it was all true.

He had formulated a plan. He was afraid to remain with his German host. It was dangerous for both. He wasn't sure just how anti-Nazi this family would be if circumstances put them to the test. Papa had heard that the authorities did not bother Jews who had a visa to another country. As far as Germany was concerned, they were considered gone—good riddance. The American Embassy had our affidavits, and Papa had an official number with the embassy. That's where, he figured, he must go.

The American Embassy did not open until 9 AM, so Papa had to use up at least two hours. He rode whatever trolleys and busses were operating, and changed from time to time so as to appear like a normal commuter and not to arouse suspicion. When it came closer to 9 o'clock, he took the bus which went into the central area and past the American Embassy. As the bus approached, he was surprised to see hundreds of people, many still in their pajamas and robes, jammed against the front and garden gates, trying to push them open. On the other side, on American soil, several people stood around watching the events, but they did not open the gates. On the fringes of the mob, Gestapo and SS men were picking up screaming and struggling figures and were dragging them to waiting trucks. It was 20 minutes before 9.

Papa continued on the bus for exactly ten more

minutes. Then he got off, crossed the street, and boarded another bus going back toward the embassy. If his calculation was correct, he would arrive there at precisely 9 AM. He did. As he stepped off the bus, the embassy gates were opened and a flood of people poured onto the grounds. There was no stopping them. The Gestapo and SS men were shoved aside and Papa joined in the mob and pushed his way through with the others. For the moment, he was on American soil, safe from German authority.

The embassy people were sympathetic and did what they could. They brought in food, allowed the pathetic crowd to stand and sit in the doorways, halls, and gardens, and tried to calm frightened adults and children. After several hours, Papa finally managed to get the attention of one of the embassy clerks. He told her that he had an official visa number and pleaded with her to arrange an appointment with an officer. The young woman reminded him that there was little work being accomplished under the circumstances, but she promised to do what she could. He never saw her again. He gave up hope. At 5 PM, the embassy was ready to close. Hundreds of people still lingered on the grounds. They refused to leave. A high-ranking American embassy official rushed out of his protective office to plead with the crowd. Papa intercepted him in the hall, grabbed his sleeve, and held on. With tears in his eyes, he told him of his visa number and begged the official to have our number changed into an actual visa there and then. The bewildered man looked at Papa, at the crowd he was about to face, back at Papa, and motioned to an assistant. "See this man now," he directed, "and if he checks out, give him his visa."

Arnold Geier with sister Ruth, mother Regina, and father Juda, in Berlin

Within an hour, Papa was the proud owner of a precious American visa. It was no more than a large rubber stamp on one page of his passport, with names and dates of birth inserted, but, in Germany on this day, it was life itself. Papa came home. On the way, he was stopped several times, showed his visa, and was left alone.

I never learned the fate of the others who had fled to the security of the American Embassy that day. Grandpa had hidden with a German family on the outskirts of the city and returned only after the pogrom had calmed down. He had an unused affidavit. He never obtained an official number for a visa, because the quota was never reopened. Grandpa, Grandma, and Aunt Dora did not survive. Thanks to Papa's determination and courage, we did.

From Darkness to Light

By Arnold Geier

BERLIN, GERMANY
MIAMI, FLORIDA

December 25, 1938 was a glorious day. The world celebrated Christmas, and even the Germans we had encountered that morning seemed almost mellow. A small segment of humanity would, that evening, celebrate the last day of Chanukah, the Jewish Festival of Lights. Our little family also celebrated a most important event—we were finally on our way out of Germany, headed toward a new life in the "Golden Land," the U.S.A.

We had survived every measure the Hitler regime had contrived against Jews, including the recent Kristallnacht, and finally had received our passport to freedom, an American visa.

Now, on this sunny but chilly day, we sat quietly in a second class compartment of the train that had left Berlin early that morning and was due to arrive in

71

Holland later that night. Two stern Germans shared the compartment with my father, mother, my 15-year-old sister, and me. I was twelve. We children peered out the window and occupied ourselves with chatter about the sights racing by. Papa was deep in thought and Mama interrupted her reading from time to time to whisper to him. I overheard her reassuring my father, a Cantor and an orthodox Jew, that, under these circumstances, God would surely forgive him for having to ignore the last day of Chanukah.

The journey was uneventful. We ate the sandwiches Mama had prepared, we dozed, we stretched our legs with occasional walks to adjoining cars, we chatted quietly so the Germans in our compartment would not be angered, and we watched the time drag by ever so slowly.

After darkness settled gently over the countryside, the train slowed and puffed its way into a special railway station at the German-Dutch border, its brakes squealing and hissing as it jerked to a stop. We braced ourselves for our final encounter with German police, Nazis, and Gestapo. Freedom was close at hand. A bit more time and a few more miles and our old lives were over. No matter what was ahead, it surely would be better.

The train sat in the station for an almost-endless ten minutes while we watched teams of Border Police officers and Gestapo agents organizing themselves with typical German efficiency on the platform for the task of checking everyone's passport and travel papers. Finally, small groups began to climb aboard. Papa looked tense and broke out in a sweat. I was afraid.

At that instant, without a flicker of warning, every light in the station and on the train went out. The area was pitch black. Noises of confusion and alarm cut through the blackness. Several people struck matches and their eerie and frightened faces suddenly sprang from the darkness, casting ghostly shadows, and quickly disappeared with the flame. I wanted to scream, but I didn't.

Papa suddenly stood up, groped around the luggage rack above him, pulled down his overcoat, and reached into one of its pockets and pulled out a small packet. He gently pushed me away from the window, struck a match, lit a candle, and, using its flame, slowly and deliberately, warmed the bottoms of eight other Chanukah candles and placed them neatly in a row on the window ledge. He then murmured the appropriate blessings as he lit each one carefully and finally planted the ninth candle slightly off to the side. He sank gently into his seat and, for the first time in a long time, I saw a smile on Papa's face.

Someone on the platform shouted: "There's light over there!" Within a few minutes, different teams of Border Police and Gestapo agents came into our compartment to check passports and papers by the flickering Chanukah lights. The chief Border Police officer, seated at the light, complimented my father for being wise enough to take along "travel candles." We discreetly left the compartment and watched the amazing scene from the passageway near the door.

After about a half hour or so, the Chanukah candles seemed to have no more than a few minutes of life left in them. Suddenly, as unexpectedly as the lights had gone off, they came on again. There was momentary shock at the harsh glow of the instant brightness, but there was also a sigh of relief. One officer curtly thanked my father, left our compartment, and joined the others who were spreading out to continue their work throughout the train.

Papa turned to me and smiled. "Remember this moment, son," he declared softly, "like in the days of the Maccabees, a great miracle happened here."

Draugas

As told by Sali Solskis—Charles Saul (Deceased)

Kovno, Lithuania
New York, New York

As far back as I can trace my family tree, there has always been a Solskis living in the Kovno area of Lithuania. The most successful one, I believe, was my grandfather. Soon after Lithuania gained its independence in 1918, he acquired several farms and a lumberyard and managed them with the help of his five sons. My father ran one of the farms where I spent the early years of my life. In my teens, I worked in the sawmill of our Kovno lumberyard which was about 20 miles west toward the German border. Lumber from Lithuanian pines was considered among the most desirable in Europe, and German furniture factories snapped up all they could buy.

In May 1940, the Russians marched into Lithuania. Just before they reached Kovno, our family stocked up on food, clothing, and other non-perishable items. Who knew what the future would hold? I hoarded my favorite cigarettes, Turkish Turmacs, which could be distinguished by their golden tips and strong aromatic flavor. They were expensive and hard to get.

The Russians nationalized everything, including the farms and lumberyards. After a few months, they fired everyone in our mill without explanation. I went to Kovno to look for work. I was a strong, friendly 20-year-old, with valuable experience. I soon found a job in one of the many Kovno sawmills. The Russians transported lumber westward for fortifications and military preparations. My specialty was measuring lumber. After my two helpers stacked the lumber, I measured each piece and listed how many cubic board-feet were being shipped, or verified specific measurements ordered by the Russians.

I always got along well with my co-workers. I would often share my sandwiches with one of my helpers, a fellow I knew only as "Draugas" ("good buddy" in Lithuanian slang). Sometimes I would even offer him one of my Turmacs. He was a poor man, and this expensive smoke was a treat. He would slap me on the back and thank me for giving him pleasure. "I'll remember you," he would assure me with a laugh.

I worked in the mill until June 1941, when the Germans invaded. After a week of combat, Lithuania was conquered.

I was home in Kovno on the afternoon of July 4th when four armed Lithuanian pro-Nazi "Partisans," in dirty green uniforms with yellow armbands, burst through the front door. All were drunk and took great pleasure in menacing us with their rifles. They rummaged through the house and took whatever they wanted. Then, at gunpoint, they ordered the males in the house to assemble outside. There were twelve of us; my father and several uncles and cousins.

They marched us for two hours to a hill, and up a path toward the top. It was a warm day, and we perspired profusely. Finally we reached a large flat surface, the size of a football field, surrounded by a tall wire fence. At the entrance stood a guardhouse, painted in the yellow, green and red colors of Lithuania, and at the far edge of the area was a shed. To our astonishment, we saw ditches, 20-30 yards long, filled with Jewish men digging slowly, methodically, and with expressions of hopelessness and resignation on their faces. There were at least 800 Jews, and they knew they were digging their own graves. The Lithuanians pushed the twelve of us into one of the ditches, threw us shovels and ordered us to dig. We had no choice, so we began to dig slowly. Why rush the inevitable?

At one point, as I brushed the perspiration from my forehead, I felt as if eyes were staring at me. I looked up. Towering above me, wearing a yellow armband and toting a rifle, was Draugas, my "buddy," from the sawmill. "Is that you, Draugas?" he called out, his speech slurred from alcohol. "Yes, Draugas," I replied. "Come up here and talk to me," he ordered. I climbed out, and he told me to sit down. I reached into my pocket, took out what was left of my last pack of Turmacs, and offered him one. He gave me a

drunken smile. "You still have those. Good." We smoked together. As I looked around, I noticed Germans in light brown shirts and pistol holsters milling about and laughing.

"What will be with us, Draugas?" I asked. "Can you help us?"

My look and plea must have penetrated the man's stupor. He leaned on his rifle to steady himself. "I told you I'll remember you," he began, "but I can't promise anything. Go into the hole now. I'll come back later." Then he turned and walked away. Would he really come back? Despair swept over me. I wished he hadn't raised my hopes. It would make the letdown so much harder.

About a half hour later, at approximately 7:30 PM, the heavens suddenly opened. Sheets of rain fell on the area. I had never seen such a deluge. It rarely rained in July, so everyone was caught by surprise. The Germans and the Lithuanian guards scrambled and raced to the shed for shelter. Then I heard a voice. "Get out, Draugas, with your people. Now is the moment. Quickly!" As the twelve of us climbed out, my "buddy" lined us up in a formation of twos, and marched us toward the guardhouse. "I can't take you beyond the gate," he shouted into my ear to overcome the sound of the rain, "stay off the sidewalk and don't talk loud. Then you are on your own." I offered him whatever money we had in our pockets, but he refused. As we reached the guardhouse, my Draugas told the Lithuanian Partisan that we were ordered to a work detail down the road. We marched on for a few minutes, and only then did I dare turn around. My Draugas was gone.

We continued walking silently. We didn't encounter anyone, only the unending deluge. By 11 o'clock, as night fell, we were soaked to the skin, but safely back in our house. We had literally returned from the grave.

During the next three years, all Jews in the area were moved into the Kovno ghetto. I worked in a construction gang that set planks in fields to create landing strips for German military planes. I knew that eventually the Germans would kill us all. My uncle Chaskel Solskis and one of his friends planned to escape into the woods and build underground shelters for their families. I decided to join them.

We worked from November 1943 to January 1944 constructing deep hidden shelters, digging sanitation facilities, and arranging for food storage and camouflage. We stole fruits and vegetables from nearby farms. But we should have gone farther into the woods. A Lithuanian Partisan patrol spotted our tracks in the snow, raided the hideaway, and captured us.

The patrol leader ordered one of his men to ride into a nearby village and borrow a sleigh and horses so that the three of us could be delivered to the Germans. The Partisan rode off, and about an hour later returned with a group of area farmers, led by the village elder. He immediately recognized my uncle. This man was one of the most respected farmers in the area and had done business with my grandfather, parents and uncles. When it had become obvious that our properties and possessions would be lost, our family had given this farmer and his relatives our machinery and animals. He turned to the Partisans. "Enough already," he said, "these are the same Jews, our Jews, that we have lived with all these years. They never did anything to us. There are so few left and we don't want their blood on our hands. Let them go their way." It was more of a command than a request. The other farmers nodded in agreement. The elder was highly regarded, and the patrol leader did not dare challenge him. He grumbled: "All right, so someone else will get them." He gave a halfhearted salute and led his men back into the forest. We thanked the villagers and left. My uncle and I split up. A few miles away, I found haven with a friendly farmer, remained there for a while, and, experiencing many close calls, made my way through the countryside toward the Russian Partisans fighting from the forests. I reached them on July 30, 1944. I was free at last.

I was not aware of what was happening to the others during their terrible existence in the ghetto. The Germans shot my brother, in front of my mother, on March 27, 1944, his 8th birthday. She was taken to Stutthof Concentration Camp from which she was later liberated by the Red Army. My father burned to death when the Germans torched the Kovno ghetto, and my uncles and cousins disappeared.

After liberation, I returned to Kovno to search for any family that may have survived. I found no one, except for my uncle who had made his way back as I did. Now, I had to work for the Russians. Because of my experience with lumber, I was provided with a motorcycle to take me into the woods to work, and I was also exempted from military duty.

The war was winding down as the Red Army

pushed deeper into Germany. I spent many days searching through the ruins of the Kovno ghetto, hoping to find a trace of my family, but there was none.

One day, after another disappointing search, I walked along the river in a sad and angry mood. As I began to cross over a bridge, I lifted my head, and my eyes fixed upon the face of a man coming toward me. He was in rags. For an instant, I saw signs of recognition, terror, panic and pleading. It was my Lithuanian Draugas, my "buddy" who loved Turkish Turmacs!

In another instant, I realized my position. Who knows how many Jews this man had killed? Who knows what other crimes he had committed? Should I turn him in to the Russians?

He "remembered" me when it meant my life, and I could not abandon him now. I knew if I spoke to him and subsequently he was picked up by the Russians, he would always believe I had betrayed him. I made my decision. I passed him by without the slightest sign of recognition. Now, my debt was paid. He was on his own. The fates would mete out whatever punishment he deserved, but not by my hand. Sometimes, the best way to "remember" is to forget.

Always Faithful

As told by Miriam Krysia Goldwasser Fellig

WARSAW, POLAND
MIAMI BEACH, FLORIDA

Marisia was part of my life from the day I was born in 1931. She was the family's governess and lived with us in our large comfortable fourth-floor apartment on fashionable Marchalkowska Street in Warsaw. For all practical purposes, she was a member of the family. In her mid-30s, a bit heavy-set and of average height, she had dark brown hair with eyes to match, and a face heavily marked from an earlier bout with smallpox.

In offices on the first floor of the same apartment building, my father, with a partner and several employees, operated an advertising agency. Often, after picking me up from school, Marisia would leave me at the office so that I could spend some time with my father. I pretended to be working with the others.

83

They humored me by giving me small tasks to perform and, with tolerant smiles, watched my serious efforts to complete them. Sometimes, I fell asleep in the office and awakened in the apartment three stories above.

I adored my father. He was a kind, energetic, optimistic, warm, and caring person. He was as considerate of his employees and other people as he was of his family. Everyone liked him. My mother was a leader of Warsaw's Jewish society ladies, spending much of her time in coffee houses and at charity parties. She enjoyed her comforts.

When the Germans invaded Poland in September 1939, my father, a captain in the Cavalry, pitted his horses against steel tanks. The horses lost. To avoid capture, he fled to Bialystok, in the Russian half of Poland. He arranged for Mother, Brother, Marisia and me to be smuggled across the border and be brought to him. But after an uncomfortable and bitter winter, and missing his mother terribly, he decided to smuggle us back to the comforts we enjoyed in Warsaw. We did not foresee what was in store for us there.

Just after we returned, the Germans ordered all Jews to move immediately into a specified area. It came to be known as the Warsaw ghetto. My father was fortunate to find someone who would exchange his small apartment in that area for our large one downtown. We moved into the crowded quarters and Marisia came with us. She cared for my brother and me while the adults were forced to work in ghetto factories. Eventually, she was forbidden to live in the area and had to move. But she got word to my father where she could be reached.

At the end of 1942, the Germans announced that all workers of certain factory complexes in the ghetto would be transported to "more suitable and comfortable quarters." My parents knew what that meant. How right they were—both soon perished at Poniatowa Concentration Camp near Lodz. They had already lost my grandmother and brother. Each was shot in an "Aktion" (purge). They knew that once they were forced out of the picture, I would probably not survive. So father devised a plan.

He knew a Jewish nurse who was allowed to come and go in order to work at a local hospital. She told him that every day a group of women would leave the ghetto to clean toilets at the hospital. They would be counted as they left the gate, and again when they returned. She had also heard of one woman who had escaped but wanted to return to the ghetto to be with her husband. I had always been large and tall for my age, so one day, I left the ghetto in the column of cleaning women, marched to the hospital, changed clothes with the woman who wanted to return, and was taken away by a waiting Marisia. She took me to the suburbs, then found a priest who was willing to sell her a birth certificate of a girl my age who had died. With this document, she was able to pass me off as her niece. She worked whenever possible to feed and house us.

One afternoon, we were walking in the street when a voice boomed pleasantly: "Panienka (Miss) Marisia, Panienka Krysia!" We froze in terror. Who recognized us? We turned slowly. It was the policeman who was posted on the corner of our street in Warsaw where we would cross on our way to and from school. He smilingly reassured Marisia that he was appalled at what was going on and wanted to help us. Marisia thanked him and gave him our address. We did not realize at that moment how foolish it was.

Five days later, three husky Polish men came to our door and forced their way in. They knew who we were and threatened to deliver us to the Gestapo unless we came up with money. This ploy was not uncommon. There was a cash bounty awaiting any Pole who brought in fugitive Jews. We pleaded with them that we simply didn't have any money and begged for mercy. It seemed to fall on deaf ears.

One of the men convinced the others to let him talk to us privately because he had a way of finding out if we were telling the truth. They left the room.

The man looked at me and asked: "Don't you remember me?" Both Marisia and I shook our heads. "I worked for your father on Marchalkowska Street," he continued, "and many a time when you would fall asleep in the office, I carried you upstairs to your apartment." We were flabbergasted. "Your father was always good to me. One time, I had some trouble and his partner wanted to fire me. But when I explained my problem, your father stood up for me and saw to it that I kept my job. Now, I want to help you. I will get you out of here, but you must never come back." He told us to get ready to leave. We took whatever we could carry without arousing suspicion and left with him. He told the others he doubted if we were the right people, but he would take us to the Gestapo to find out. He put us into a small car, drove off, and let us out after a few minutes.

Marisia took me deep into the countryside and arranged for me, her twelve-year-old "niece", to be cared for in a convent. I remained there for several months. Of course, nobody knew I was Jewish. I noticed another little girl who was exceptionally quiet and serious. We never spoke to each other, yet, I thought, we both knew what we were. Then I fell ill, and the nuns notified Marisia they could no longer take care of me.

She took me to a cousin with whom she had not been in contact for many years. She introduced me as her child out of wedlock. As unpleasant as this admission was to her religious cousin, she allowed us to rent a room in an apartment she was renting to a prostitute who made homemade whiskey on the side to supplement her income. She and Marisia made an arrangement whereby Marisia would hide the whiskey in a basket under some slaughtered chickens, take them to Warsaw, sell them, and split the profits. That's how we stayed alive. I had to remain in bed to recuperate, but I could hear the train whistle, and knew it would take twenty minutes for Marisia to arrive from the station and open my door. But I always lived in fear she would be caught and that door would not open.

In early 1944, the Russians liberated us. Marisia took me to a sister in Lodz, again passing me off as her out-of-wedlock child. When the American Joint Distribution Committee opened an office there and called for anyone who knew of survivors to come forward, Marisia urged me to register as a Jewish orphan. I refused because I didn't want to leave her. I could not imagine life alone, without her. But she insisted and I finally gave in. That is how a relative in Canada found me. I was moved to a Jewish orphanage in France, where, incidentally, I met the sad and silent little girl

Miriam and Marisia in hiding

from the convent again. Then I was sent to Canada to start a new life.

For many years, I tried to get Marisia into Canada. This faithful, caring person was not "family" and therefore did not qualify. I sent her letters and packages and kept in touch. I planned to visit her with my children when they were old enough to travel and understand, but by then it was too late. She had passed away peacefully in Poland.

If there are angels, she is one. If there is a heaven, she is there.

The Girl in the K.L. Dress

As told by George Katzman

MIAMI, FLORIDA

It was almost over. German forces were on the run everywhere. My unit, the 16th Tank Battalion, U. S. Army, was part of a lightning push across the slice of Nazi territory still unconquered. We were heading toward Pilsen, Czechoslovakia, about 75 miles away. I was a 25-year-old GI on combat patrol to spot areas of possible resistance or danger in the path of the tanks.

We intercepted a convoy of German trucks, and our tanks put them under a barrage of fire. Through my field glasses, I could see people, mostly civilians, jumping off the vehicles and frantically running toward the woods. Little did I know that one of them was my 17-year-old daughter-to-be.

Three weeks later, the war was over. There were still small pockets of resistance and we continued our combat patrols. On a narrow Czech side road, I came upon two scrawny girls. They were so emaciated, it was hard to judge their ages. They wore ragged dresses, marked with the letters K.L. stamped across the front in white. As I approached, unshaven and with grenades hanging from my shoulders, I could see the fear in their eyes. I tried to relax them with light conversation. In halting German, I said to the taller one, "Bitte, Fraulein, was ist das K.L.?" She hesitated, and with a quiver in her voice answered, "It means Konzentrations Lager. Concentration Camp. We are Jews." They were startled when my face broke into a giant smile. I quickly reassured them that there was nothing to fear, and that I, too, was a Jew. They began to relax and told me they were on their way from Auschwitz to Vienna on the truck convoy my unit had shelled. They had escaped into the woods during the bombardment, and stayed in hiding for a week. Then the war ended, but they had nowhere to go. They made their way to a little village and found temporary shelter.

The Captain interrupted: "Katzman, cut the chatter and let's get moving!" As I drove off, I waved and had a last look at the two pathetic children standing barefooted, with ugly malnutrition sores visible through their tattered little dresses. I wondered what would become of them.

During the next few days, our outfit moved out of Pilsen and closer to the German border. The area, known as Sudetenland, was populated by over three million ethnic Germans, most of whom were ardent Nazi supporters. One afternoon, a Jewish soldier from my unit came by as I was cleaning my rifle. "George," he said, "a buddy of mine told me there are a couple

of Jewish kids holed up in the town down the road."
He pointed in the direction of the area I had patrolled
a week earlier. My interest was stirred. "Let's check it
out," I suggested. I quickly finished cleaning the rifle
and loaded it, and the two of us started out on foot.
From time to time, fanatic hold-outs still sniped at
American soldiers, so our rifles stayed loaded.

We reached the village, with its typical church in
the main square, a few streets leading to the square,
and a duck pond at the far end. Near the pond, I
looked up at a window and there she was—the little
girl with the K.L. dress. Her face lit up when our eyes
met. "What are you doing here?" she asked excitedly.
"We're looking for you," I responded with joy in my
voice and heart. "Come in, please come in," she motioned toward the entrance.

The room was small and bare, except for a large
bed and some chairs. There were three girls—my
"girl," Helena, age 17, her red-headed friend Agnes,
age 16, and Heidi, age 19, who was sick in bed. They
felt comfortable with us because we were Jewish, and
reluctantly told their story; they lost their parents, survived Auschwitz, escaped into the woods after the convoy was shelled, and made their way to the village.
But, the kind Czech who sheltered them had told them
he would need the room in a few days for a relative
who was returning from the war. We decided we
would take them back to our village the next day.

I picked up the girls and, on the way back, drove
them to an Army hospital to have them examined. Helena
and Agnes had no serious problems and were reassured
that a better diet would improve their health. But Heidi
was kept there for heart examinations and treatment.

As we approached our village, I stopped at the nicest house I could spot, and banged on the front door. A fat Sudeten German, an unhappy frown on his face, greeted me with a gruff "what do you want?" Purposefully grasping my rifle, I ordered him to accompany me on an inspection of the house. It had three rooms with a kitchen that could be closed off as an apartment. "Remove all your personal things from these rooms in five minutes!" I barked. "I'm bringing you guests." Without another word, I left.

Helena and Agnes were bewildered by their new luxurious surroundings. While they were unpacking the few boxes with their belongings, I went to the local police barracks three doors away. In German, I told the girls' story to the Czech Partisans, who were patrolling the area, and asked them to keep a sharp eye on my charges. They were eager to cooperate. One gave me a radio he had "liberated" and three accompanied me back to the house. While I was installing the radio and enjoying the evident delight of Helena and Agnes, the Partisans were having a forceful and intense "conference" with the owner of the house. There would be no problems, I was sure.

At my own billet, I called a few of the Jewish GIs together and told them about my girls. Mess Sergeant Bill Feder rounded up some food, and others dug through their duffle bags and lockers for anything that could be useful to the young survivors.

That night, nine rugged American combat veterans sat on the floor at the feet of the two children, watching them devouring the meats, fruits and sweets, with pleasure and joy. It was undoubtedly the best they had eaten in years. On that night was born my attachment to my special child, Helena. I was to be her father, counselor, nurse, comforter and protector for the next two months.

From then on, buddies from our unit helped me "liberate" shoes, clothing, bicycles, and small luxury items that would please the girls. Their teeth were fixed, courtesy of a sympathetic military dentist who proclaimed himself to be the "U.S. Army Clandestine Dental Division." Heidi was released from the hospital and joined her friends. In the evening, those who were off duty would drop by to "cheer up our kids." Although they were often moody and depressed, the girls' physical well-being improved dramatically. Their malnutrition sores began to heal, as their bony cheeks filled out, and their eyes lost their hollow shells and looked rested and, sometimes, even mischievous.

No father took greater delight in his child than I did. I watched Helena primp in new dresses we had "persuaded" a tailor to make for the girls from "liberated" cloth. Her cheeks turned youthfully rosy, and her smile became more frequent and brighter. But I knew it could not last.

I heard that our unit would be disbanded and we would be sent to other outfits or to the Pacific war area. Then our kids would be at the mercy of the Sudeten Germans, many of whom were still Nazis and would willfully harm them. I estimated we had two weeks to do something.

I called my buddies together to plan some action. Marriage was out—we were still at war with Japan and, besides, Army regulations prohibited marriages in a forward zone. We requested adoption papers but were immediately turned down.

Agnes (front), Hedi, and Helena after recuperation

We wrote our parents to contact high authorities in New York and Washington to begin adoption procedures. They too were turned down. We were stymied and frantic, and had lost ten days.

The First Sergeant then had an idea: "Katzman, why don't you ask for help from the Red Cross in Pilsen?" I hopped into my jeep and left.

I had heard that the woman in charge was a sympathetic person. I barged in on her, steered her toward a corner where we could talk without being overheard, and blurted out the story of my three little girls and their problem. "They'll kill them for sure if we pull out and just leave them." The woman's eyes showed her sympathy and concern. She leaned forward. "There may be a way," she whispered. "The Jewish Haganah has been able to smuggle a few youngsters from the nearby camp, run by the United Nations Relief and Rehabilitation Administration (UNRRA), through the British lines at Salzburg, Austria, and from there to Palestine and safety. Do you want me to initiate arrangements?" "What if they are caught?" I asked. She explained that they would be returned to the dreary existence at the UNRRA camp, but at least there would be no danger to their lives. I pressed her hands, expressed my deep gratitude, and eagerly accepted her offer of help.

The next morning, I called my buddies together and gave them the news. They started to prepare packages of food and clothing, while I went to the house and invited Helena for a stroll, as we had done so often before.

"Helena," I began, "I just returned from Pilsen where I made some arrangements for you and the girls." She stopped in her tracks and her face turned pale. She stared to weep softly. "I knew it wouldn't last," she sobbed, "the happiness was too much. What will become of us now?" She wrung her hands like an old lady. "What will become of us?"

Gently, I explained the events of the past two weeks. When I told her of our unsuccessful attempts to adopt the three of them, she broke down and cried somberly. We were the only family she had left. My heart was breaking. Finally, I told her about the plan to bring them to the UNRRA camp and eventually to Palestine. Her tears dried and she seemed to go emotionally dead—she felt deserted and stranded. "When do we go?" she asked in a hollow voice. "Tomorrow."

That afternoon was filled with gloom as nine of us crowded into the small flat. We gave them food, shoes, clothes, money, photographs, bikes, and suitcases. In addition, we prepared stamped envelopes addressed to us at home and asked them to write as soon as they could. Gloom and sadness overpowered everyone. Very little was said to break the silence.

A U.S. Army truck pulled up the following day, and we helped load the boxes and suitcases. These were probably the wealthiest refugees who ever left for a UNRRA camp. They were also the most miserable. We hugged and held each other and said our goodbyes and, when the loaded truck pulled away, I stood in the middle of the road, a broad smile on my face, and a cheerful wave of my arm. The minute they were swallowed by the horizon, my legs buckled, and I sat on the dirt road and cried for the first time since I was 10.

People stared at me, but I didn't care—I had just lost my daughter and I knew it was forever.

For the next five years, I tried to find Helena, my little girl, but without success. No letter ever came from her. Every government and humanitarian agency I contacted was unable to help. In 1950, I decided to move to Europe for a year and try to find her. While looking in vain for a daughter, I found, instead, a wife in Paris. We returned to New York and I resumed my life as an engineer.

One afternoon in 1952, I received a call at the office from my wife. She was almost hysterical. She had just heard from Helena. After seven years of searching, I would see my daughter in my home that night at 7 PM! I was overjoyed.

When the door opened, there stood a tall, beautiful girl, chic in the latest style, posed and gracious, returning to my life. It was a wonderful reunion. Indeed, she had written and mailed the envelope I had provided, but the postage I had used was not valid. Helena eventually came to America from a Displaced Persons camp in Italy. She settled in New York, married, had children, and became a fashion designer. One day, she found the photograph I had given her with my mother's phone number on the back. Although so many years had passed, she tried it anyway. Of course, she didn't know that my mother had passed away a year earlier, that we had moved into her house and retained her number. That's why, when Helena called, my wife was there to answer.

It was meant to be—just as I was meant to be on a dirt road in Czechoslovakia, finding the emaciated little girl in the K.L. dress.

Helena today

George Katzman today

Special Delivery

As told by Anna Rabinowicz Dichter

BORYSLAV, POLAND
BROOKLYN, NEW YORK

The war was almost over for me, but I didn't know that. In fact, I had my doubts that it would ever end. After almost three years of facing terror, fright, alarm and hunger, my only thoughts were of survival. For my mother, it was too late. She had been taken away early in the Nazi occupation of Boryslav, our small town in Poland. My father had been in a labor camp just outside town until a few days ago when the Germans disbanded the camp and shipped all inmates to death camps. Father never returned. My younger sister was hidden somewhere in the area, and my husband Bronek, my 8-year-old son Wilhelm, and I were huddled, sick, hungry and desperate, in a tiny attic room, our fifth hiding place. The bed was our table, chair, playground and hospital—the center of our very existence.

During the dark chilly nights of April 1944, I was often unable to sleep. I would sit on the edge of our small bed and watch my sleeping son breathe with heaviness interrupted by occasional sighs. I wondered if he would some day be able to play the games that children play and if he would ever learn to smile. He had been cooped up in small rooms for over two years. His muscles were turning stiff.

My gaze and thoughts would turn to my husband as he tried to stifle an oncoming cough or bury his head in the pillow to muffle the sound. A severe cold had developed into tuberculosis just before the Germans arrived. At night, there were no outside noises to absorb the echoes of his persistent, racking coughs. Often, he would break into an uncontrollable sweat which bathed him from head to toe. I could only try to dry his brow and whisper words of comfort. For us, there was no doctor, no medication, no help from anyone. Once, my husband begged me to let him leave, arguing that his absence would make my movements with Wilhelm easier.

"Bronek Rabinowicz," I had said in stern tones, "I will have none of that kind of talk. We are together and will remain together no matter what. I need you and Wilhelm needs you and we will make it, together!" I must have sounded convincing. Bronek never brought the subject up again.

One evening in late April, our "landlord" brought us some food and with it, he handed me a letter. It was from my sister. It had been given to him by a co-worker at the plant, who was hiding Irene.

I trembled with joy and fear. This was only the second time I heard from my sister since she went underground two years earlier. Why did she write and risk betrayal and capture? It had to be important. I secretly wished I would not have to open the envelope. But I did. Irene was despondent. She had learned that our father was gone. We were the only ones left in the family. If anything happened to me, she wrote, she would not want to live. We had always been close and even now, as a 20-year-old, she looked up to me, eight years her senior, and depended on me for strength. She desperately wanted to see me, even if only for a couple of days. She would send someone to bring me to her soon.

Bronek and I agonized about my sister's cry. It would be very dangerous to go to her. I might be seen and recognized. I might be prevented from returning. But we could not ignore her plea, and I also longed to be with her again. Bronek understood. We decided I would take the chance.

In the late afternoon of May 2, 1944, there was a soft knock on our hidden door. A thin, tall, emaciated young man introduced himself as Moshko. He had come to take me to Irene. He explained that he was also Jewish and was in hiding with her. My sister's talk of suicide had moved him to come for me. We waited for darkness. Just as I was ready to leave, my son grabbed my arm and wouldn't let go. "Take me with you, Mama!" he sobbed. "Please, Mama, I want to go with you!" My heart cried out to him. "Wilhelm, my darling. How will you walk? You haven't walked in three years. I can't carry you. It's too far." There was a tear in Moshko's eye. "I'll carry him."

He extended his scrawny arms as if to receive a package. My husband also pleaded with me to take our son. "How often can he see his aunt?" he argued. "I'll be safe here. Wilhelm will be better off with you." With heavy heart, I agreed. We packed a few personal items, and in a separate paper, I wrapped a gift for my sister—an onion and a bulb of garlic. It was all I had. Moshko picked up my son and gently lifted him onto his back.

Once outside, my mind was occupied with the surroundings. We had to get to the edge of town as quickly as possible. Not only was there danger of being recognized as Jews, but all civilians were forbidden on the streets when curfew began at dusk. We took back roads and walked across fields for hours. We encountered no one. Tiny house lights on the edge of Boryslav could be seen in the distance.

Suddenly, we heard the sound of an airplane overhead, apparently approaching Boryslav from the Russian side. Sirens blared and beams of searchlights crisscrossed the sky over the town. I was stunned. During the three years of war, we had never even seen a Russian plane. We stopped for a few minutes and watched. Were they after the nearby oil fields? Why only one plane? The small plane winged its way over Boryslav and dropped one bomb. There was one explosion and, in a few minutes, the plane was gone, the sirens were silent, and the sky was black again. The sudden quiet jolted us back to reality and we resumed walking.

At about 2 o'clock in the morning, we crossed a field and approached a small farmhouse. Moshko stopped, listened intently, and motioned us on. We carefully skirted the house and came upon a grassy area, at the end of which I could see the outline of a stone well, about five feet in diameter. When we reached it, Moshko, to my utter amazement, lifted himself and my son on his back over the wall, and disappeared into the well. A few moments later, he returned alone, took me by the hand and led me to the opening. Then I understood. The inner circumference of the well was made of rocks. Approximately four feet down the side of the well there was an opening in the wall. Moshko gripped my hands and told me to climb down toward the barely visible opening. I was petrified. I braced myself against the rocks so as not to fall into ten feet of water, slowly inched my way down until my toes could feel firmness under them.

I swung into the area and to my joy and astonishment faced my sister in a cavern, probably not larger than four by six feet, dug into the side of the well. She had been hiding there with Moshko and another man. They depended on her "landlord," the owner of the house, to bring some food at night.

We fell into each others arms, cried sweet and bitter tears, and talked through much of the night while my son and the others fell into a sleep of exhaustion. Eventually, Irene and I also nodded off, amidst a feeling of euphoria.

In the morning, we were awakened by the insistent call of Irene's name from the opening of the well. My sister was alarmed. It was her "landlord." He had never come to the well during daylight. She stuck her head through the opening and looked up. The landlord was apprehensive and nervous. "Irene," he started, "last night a Russian plane dropped one single

bomb on Boryslav. It hit one house. When the firemen came, they found one person in the house, dead. It was your brother-in-law Bronek Rabinowicz. I thought you should know." With that he left.

The memory of that day still haunts me. Here I was in an enclave in the ground with my son and sister, safe and sound, and only a few hours earlier I was with my beloved husband, discussing whether to heed my sister's urgent summons, whether to take Wilhelm with me, and rejoicing in the expectation of being together again in a couple of days.

I will never know why my sister sent for me on that particular day; why a plane dropped a single bomb to end the life of a 36-year-old man riddled with tuberculosis; and how the rest of our little family could survive in that hole in the well until liberation, which came three months later. But survive we did and all of us made new lives for ourselves, hopeful for the future, but forever bound to the past.

The Angels of Frankfurt

As told by Elfriede Morgenstern Zundell

FRANKFURT, GERMANY
CORAL GABLES, FLORIDA

For the Jews of Germany, Kristallnacht (The Night of the Broken Glass) was like an earthquake. Its powerful tremors were felt all over the country. Many lost their property, their freedom, or their lives. Synagogues, schools and stores were set ablaze. When the tremors eventually subsided, the very foundation of the Jewish existence in Germany had been irreparably damaged. It was the beginning of the Nazi's "final solution" to their "Jewish problem."

Early in the morning following that infamous night of November 9, 1938, we were awakened by loud knocking and pounding on the front door of our house, in a middle-upper class neighborhood of Frankfurt. We could hear talking, laughing, and cursing in the street. The pounding on the door didn't let up. My mother grabbed a robe, threw it over her shoulders and opened the door. Several toughs, dressed in brown shirts and armed with clubs, barged in.

"Where is the Jew Morgenstern?" they screamed. Mother fearfully explained that my father was out of town on business and was expected back in a few days. "You lie, you Jewish swine!" With that, the men swung their clubs, knocking over whatever was in their paths. Debris of glass, china and furniture flew everywhere. They rushed from room to room, searching for my father—under beds, in closets, behind furniture, and any other place a human could hide—smashing things as they went along. With anger and fury in their voices, the men finally left. "We'll get him!" was their parting shot. My little sister Sylvia and I, gripped with fear and horror, had hidden in a small sewing room when the raid began. As it got louder and violent, we could no longer hear our mother. We were sure they had killed her. When we came out of hiding, there was Mother, holding herself up against a wall, pale with fright. We began to shake and cry. This was our first experience with sheer terror.

The toughs, accompanied by a small mob, ran to the house next to ours and banged continuously on the door. In a garage apartment in back of that house lived a woman, Frau Storch, and her 12-year-old son Walter. We hardly knew them beyond a cordial greeting when our paths occasionally crossed. She heard the racket and came along the side of the building to the front of the house to see what was going on. Confronted, she confirmed that Mr. Morgenstern often traveled and that she had not seen him for several days.

As the mob moved on to make similar stops at

homes on both sides of the street, my father's car pulled up in front of our house. He had heard on the radio about "the legitimate expression of outrage of the German people against the Jews" and was worried about his family. He could not have arrived at a worse moment. Suddenly, Frau Storch ran to his car. "They are looking for you, Herr Morgenstern. Get away now before it is too late," she pleaded. He thanked her warmly and drove off. He went into hiding at the home of an old German friend and customer in the outskirts of Frankfurt.

After a few days, it became known that any Jew who possessed a visa to another country would not be detained. A person with a visa was considered to have already emigrated.

Father had been in touch with a distant cousin in the United States and had pleaded for papers for his family. The cousin, however, would vouch only for my father. He argued that times were bad and he could not assume financial responsibility, as required by American immigration laws, for the whole family. Let Father come to America, and work and save to bring the others later. Having no other choice, my father had obtained a visa to the U.S.

With much apprehension, he reported to the local police station, and this visa saved him from arrest or harm. He took no chances, remained in hiding and immediately booked passage on a German liner leaving Hamburg the following week. In the middle of one night just before sailing, he returned home, packed a suitcase, tearfully and tenderly hugged and kissed us, and assured us that we would soon be together again. We stood at the window and watched him drive away.

He left his family, his business, his town, and his country to stay alive.

Mother managed to keep the family together and functioning. A few months later, we were forced to leave our home and to move into a "Jewish area," a ghetto without walls. In addition, all our assets and personal belongings were confiscated. We were assigned a small room within the apartment of an older Jewish couple on the mezzanine level of a multi-story building. We continued our schooling, while Mother was assigned to work in a bookbindery. Although this gave her some income, she was unable to be with us when we needed her. Even on her day off, she had to attend to the necessary duties of surviving.

One of these duties was to obtain ration books to purchase clothing. Winter was approaching and she wanted to obtain warm items for us girls. While she stood in line at the ration book office awaiting her turn, an attractive young woman approached. Erika was her name, she said, and the man who distributed the ration books was her boyfriend. For a price, she could arrange for extra books for more clothes. "Are you interested?"

Mother was thrilled for the opportunity. But she expressed fear that she might get caught or questioned about the additional books. Erika asked Mother for the approximate measurements of her 9 and 6-year-old daughters and assured her she would obtain winter clothes for us. She wrote her address on a slip of paper and told Mother to send us to her the following afternoon.

The next day, after school, Sylvia and I found Erika's apartment building. It was about halfway between our school and the room where we lived. Being the older sister, I held Sylvia's hand as we climbed to the top floor of the six-story walk-up. We knocked on Erika's door. When it opened, there stood a beautiful, tall, blond lady of about 29, a big smile on her face. We took to her instantly, and the feeling seemed mutual. As soon as we entered her small one-bedroom flat, she prepared hot chocolate and cookies. It was manna from heaven. We spent over an hour with her, trying on warm sweaters, snow suits, mittens, and similar items. Erika invited us to come again after school the next day. We were delighted.

Our visits became a weekly routine. We marveled at her comfortable lifestyle. Erika always had plenty of food, her apartment was warm, her closet was filled with silky gowns, robes, and dainty negligees. And there was that pleasant scent of musk in the air. She showed us her photo album where she appeared in glamorous poses, often with young and older men, and she allowed us to use her make-up and high heels to play "grown up." We were never concerned when, from time to time, she would send us home after one of her many boyfriends arrived. We knew we would be with her again the next week. Mother listened to our excited tales after every visit, but she never explained to us why Erika had so many wonderful things brought to her by so many male friends. At my age, I wouldn't have understood what a prostitute was, anyway.

The kids from the Hitler Youth often waited for the students of our school to leave the grounds. Then, if they could catch them, they beat them up. Sylvia and I were good runners and fled to Erika's place. Every so

often, Erika came to the school to pick us up and escort us to the safety of her apartment.

Erika left our young lives as suddenly as she had entered them. The boyfriend who was in charge of ration stamp books was drafted into the Wehrmacht, and his successor at the office discovered thousands of the stamp books missing. They had been sold illegally. Erika was quickly linked to the culprit, and she was arrested. We missed her terribly.

The school closed down, winter approached, food was getting scarcer, and we had to stay in our unheated room while Mother was at work. As it got colder, we wore the clothes Erika had picked out for us to keep warm. We never took them off. We slept in them, played in them, cried in them. Without them, we would have frozen to death. Yes, we missed her terribly indeed.

At that time, my sister and I were unaware of another person involved in our lives. Every so often, Mother would give us a potato or some vegetables. She would caution us not to mention these treats to anyone. Although we didn't understand why, we promised to do so. Only later did we learn the story.

One evening, long after Sylvia and I had fallen asleep, my mother heard what sounded like a scratching against her window. She peered out and saw a female figure motioning for her to come out. Mother did. There, much to her amazement, was Frau Storch, the neighbor who had warned my father away during Kristallnacht.

Her son Walter was with her. Somehow, she had found out where we lived. She told my mother that every weekend she went to the suburbs where she cultivated a small plot of land. There she raised potatoes and vegetables to supplement her meager food supply. She took the risk of being seen in a Jewish area at night and brought a few potatoes and greens for us. My mother was moved to tears. Frau Storch pressed her hand, wished us well, and said she or little Walter would come again, if possible, in a week. It would be very late at night and she would signal the same way. She warned my mother to be careful and not to mention this even to the Jews living in the building. They might resent her good fortune and turn her in.

Frau Storch or her son came faithfully until the night before we left Frankfurt. It would have been difficult, if not impossible, to survive without her weekly gift of sustenance.

My father, meanwhile, did everything he could to get us out. He sent proper papers to the American Consulate in Stuttgart, and, as a result, we were summoned there for interrogation and examination. This entailed great trouble and expense for us, but, of course, we followed through. Unfortunately, the consulate seemed to do everything in its power not to issue the needed visas. Once we were rejected because of a cavity in one of my teeth, and another time because the validity of some paper had expired. In April 1941, we were finally issued our visas.

We were sent to Berlin by train. There, together with a few other emigres, we were put into a train compartment which was locked. We remained seated upright in that car for the long journey across Germany, through France, Spain, and into Portugal. At certain stops, food was passed to us through the window. We were released in Lisbon. There, with additional funds sent by my father and with the help of H.I.A.S. (Hebrew Immigrant Aid Society), we obtained passage on a ship to the United States. Within three weeks, our family was reunited. It was a joyous time.

Years later, I returned to Frankfurt to find Erika and Frau Storch and her son. There was no trace of any of them. Their memory may eventually be buried under the sands of time and history, but not as long as I am alive.

Thicker Than Water

As told by Elisabeth Spitzer

Vienna, Austria
Pembroke Pines, Florida

Elsa Meyer was one of my mother's oldest and dearest friends. They grew up in the same Vienna neighborhood, went to school together and shared each other's experiences, pleasant and painful, over the years.

Elsa married a Christian prior to World War I. In the enlightened, sophisticated Vienna of that time, a mixed marriage was not uncommon. Few paid attention to it, and religion was not important to the young couple. Were they happy? That's what counted. And Elsa was very happy.

Her husband eventually was drafted into the Army, was severely wounded and discharged. Their son Wilhelm was born in 1918, and Fritz came along in 1920. The children were still infants when their father succumbed to his war injuries. Elsa's mother moved in with her to help with the children. They lived on Elsa's small pension allotted to widows, and her meager earnings from temporary jobs as a legal secretary. The two women devoted themselves completely to the boys. They were determined to provide them with a practical education. They wanted to guide them toward "the good life."

This became an elusive goal. The 1934 assassination of Chancellor Dollfuss by Nazi elements, the rise to power by Chancellor Schuschnigg, his determination to crush the aggressive Nazi agitators, and the threats of Hitler's Germany all threw tiny Austria into turmoil and fear.

Elsa Meyer had a sister in Turkey who, with her husband, owned a successful rug factory. They urged Elsa to bring her family and live and work with them. The temptation was great, but Elsa decided to send only Wilhelm. He had just completed Gymnasium, the preparatory school for college, and she felt that learning a trade would be most practical under the circumstances. Fritz was due to finish Gymnasium in June of 1938, and that would be a good time for them to join Wilhelm in Turkey.

Her plans were abruptly changed by the German annexation of Austria in March 1938—The Anschluss. Nazi troops crossed into Austria. Adolf Hitler drove through Vienna, to the open adulation and cheers of the populace, his first conquest successfully completed.

Elsa's Viennese neighbors rounded up Jews and forced them to clean the sidewalks with toothbrushes.

Nobody seemed aware that the two women were Jewish. They were not bothered, but had to stand by and watch with fear and terror in their hearts as other Jews, including prominent business and professional people, were spat upon, degraded and humiliated in the streets.

Elsa Meyer quickly wrote to her son Wilhelm, requesting that he break off communication with her until the situation toned down. She did not want to call attention to herself with connections to a foreign country. In addition, Fritz was about to be graduated from Gymnasium, and his application to the University of Vienna was pending.

Fritz never made it to the University. Immediately after graduation, he was drafted into the German Army and, because he was educated, was sent to Officers Training School. When he returned to Vienna for a short leave after his graduation as an infantry officer, he found his former apartment occupied by a new family. He learned that the two women who used to live there had been arrested. Nobody knew more than that.

He kept quiet. There was nothing he could do anyway. It would be foolish, he reasoned, to establish a connection between the women and a German officer. All would suffer. He returned to his unit, and saw his first combat during the invasion of Holland. After that, he fought on various northern, western, and southern fronts. He was a strong leader and courageous officer.

When the war in Italy was winding down in early 1945, Fritz was stationed near Bergamo at Lake Como, not far from the Swiss border. One evening, a

German truck arrived from the front. A British Army patrol had been captured and was being taken to the rear. The prisoners were marched into a large tent, and an armed guard was stationed at its entrance. A German corporal walked over to Lieutenant Meyer's tent and, saluting smartly, reported his arrival. Fritz ordered: "Tell the British officer in charge I want him here in 15 minutes."

Precisely 15 minutes later, the man appeared. He wore a dirty brown uniform, torn in several places, and mud-caked boots. His face was thin and almost hidden by a scraggly, unkempt beard. He stood stiffly in the entry flap of the dimly lighted tent. "Come in," Fritz ordered. The British officer stepped forward, stopped near the small table that served as a desk, and saluted. "Captain Wilhelm Meyer reporting, Sir." It seemed to take several seconds for this pronouncement to penetrate Fritz's consciousness. His mouth fell open. Could it be possible?

It was. Fritz carefully began to identify himself. He had to be certain they were not overheard. An emotional reunion was out of the question. Wilhelm was astonished. When war clouds swept over Europe, he had made his way to England and volunteered his services. He fought in several campaigns. This was his first face-to-face encounter with the enemy. And there stood his brother, whom he had not seen in nine years, in the uniform of the German Wehrmacht. After a few minutes, all restraints vanished from the minds of both men. Their hearts took over. They embraced and hugged each other. Wilhelm revealed that he had inquired about their mother and grandmother and it was believed they had been taken to a concentration camp somewhere in Germany. He did not know if they were still alive. Fritz brought his brother up to date on the events leading to that moment, and then outlined what he planned to do the following day.

After breakfast, Fritz told one of his own men to bring a truck to the prison tent. When the English soldiers climbed aboard, he ordered the driver to take them to the Swiss border, drop them off there, and report back to him personally. "Yes, Sir" replied the soldier, climbed into the truck and drove away. As Fritz watched, a lanky figure on the truck rose and held a long salute. Fritz returned it. He thought he could see a smile penetrating the figure's thick beard.

Within a few weeks, the war was over. Fritz was demobilized and returned to Vienna. As soon as civil-

ian foreign mail service was reestablished, he contacted the British Army to see if Wilhelm had made it into Switzerland. They confirmed that he had, indeed, and gave Fritz his address.

The brothers kept in touch regularly from then on. Together, they asked various international and local organizations for information about their mother and grandmother. They verified that both women were murdered in Bergen-Belsen Concentration Camp.

Wilhelm contracted lung cancer soon after the war. He visited Fritz in Vienna several times and, in 1961, came again, this time to die. Fritz finally realized the goal he had hoped to attain in 1938—he was accepted to the Engineering School of the University of Vienna. He completed his studies with honors, married and raised a family, and achieved a high post in the Austrian government.

The Unexpected Refuge

As told by Ruth Vogel Schwarz

DRESDEN, GERMANY
POMPANO BEACH, FLORIDA

Hitler's Nuremberg Laws of 1935, directed primarily against Jews, severely restricted the business, civic and social activities of those not considered to be pure "Aryans." These edicts were prophetic of the calamity to come.

Our family lived comfortably in Dresden, Germany, where my parents had settled from Poland when they were children. Father owned three businesses, dealing in dry goods. Mother was busy taking care of me and my brothers David and Santo. We had uncles, aunts, and cousins in our neighborhood, and we were close with all of them. Early in 1936, my uncle and his family suddenly decided to move to Italy. They suspected they may have violated some of the economic decrees of the Nuremberg Laws and didn't want to be around if and when the issue came under scrutiny. After teary goodbyes, my aunt, uncle and their two daughters left Dresden and settled in Trieste.

I missed my cousins. We had been great friends. I was 13 then, Gerda was about the same age, and Helga was two years younger. We had gotten along beautifully and had shared our closest secrets as we grew into adolescence. I would listen attentively when my father read the letters from Trieste describing the peaceful and undisturbed life my relatives were able to lead.

In the spring of 1937, my uncle urged my parents to consider moving to Trieste. He suggested my father visit the city and see if he would want to relocate. After some discussion, Father decided to make the trip. I begged, cried and pleaded for him to take me along so I could see my cousins again. He reluctantly agreed.

My uncle wrote to urge Father to bring not only his own passport, but those of other members of our family. He reported that someone in Trieste was selling visas, and it couldn't hurt to have one stamped into the passports. My father relayed this suggestion to our relatives in Dresden, and some gave him their passports to take along.

We spent six glorious weeks in Trieste. Of course, my time was spent with Gerda and Helga, playing in the grass, laughing and giggling as young girls often do. Meanwhile, my uncle led my father to someone in the Bolivian Embassy who was selling visas for $10 each. My father had all the passports in his possession stamped. Not to be outdone by the Bolivians, a functionary at the Embassy of Uganda was selling visas for $8 each. So my father had the passports stamped again by the emissary from Uganda. It may turn out to be a waste of money, he reasoned, but it couldn't hurt, and you never know . . . When it was time to return to Dresden, I was overcome by sadness. Although I felt happy to have seen Gerda and Helga, I wondered silently when I would ever see them again.

In October 1938, Father and one of my uncles went to Berlin to see if they could obtain an American visa. At the embassy, they were advised they would need an affidavit from an American citizen-sponsor and, even if they had it, it was too late—the Polish quota was filled weeks earlier and was now closed.

While the two men were in Berlin, an SS man came to our home and ordered my mother to report immediately with her three children to the Dresden Police Station for passport checks. She quickly washed our hands and faces, made us go to the toilet, and hurried with us to the station. There were hundreds of grim-faced and frightened people milling about. Most, like my mother, had come in the clothes they wore when summoned. As the afternoon approached, others arrived, gripping suitcases of various sizes. Soon, it became known that everyone would be deported to Poland the next day. My mother, alone with her children, became panic-stricken, cried and fainted several times while we children looked on in helplessness and terror. We spent the night on the floor of the police station.

The following morning, an SS man brought the throng to order. "All Jews with a valid visa in their passports, report to the window at the far right corner," he bellowed. As a few people began to move from their places, Mother suddenly remembered the Bolivian and Ugandan visas Father had purchased in Italy. Could they still be valid? Would the Nazis accept them as authentic? She quickly checked. Yes! Both were good for another six months! She held my hand tightly, and with apprehension and fear, she joined the small group assembled in front of the little window. Within the hour, we were released and returned home!

In November, things got worse. When my father saw the burning synagogues, the looted stores and the violence of the foreboding Kristallnacht, he knew he had to act quickly to save himself and his family. At that particular time, The Society of Friends, commonly called The Quakers, were organizing transports to bring children from the potential war zones to the safety of England, where sympathetic families would care for them until the danger passed. Father applied to have my two brothers and me join the exodus. David and I were accepted. Little Santo, only six, was too young to qualify.

I'll never forget our last hour together. We joined dozens of children on the rail station platform. Representatives of The Quakers arranged the loading of luggage, took constant roll calls and moved groups of children in front of the specific railroad cars they would occupy. Parents talked with their youngsters, outwardly radiating cheerfulness, hope, and courage. Father gave me last minute instructions. "Keep an eye on your brother David. Always stay together. I will try to contact a cousin in London. If I am successful, he will surely come for you. Remember this is only temporary. We will join you as soon as possible." As boarding time was announced, the facade of bravery quickly disappeared, and we all clung to each other, tears running down our faces. Finally, Father, Mother and Santo escorted David and me to our compartment, and after some last-minute strong hugs returned

to the platform to watch us depart toward a new life without them. They waved and cried as the train pulled out, and soon they were out of sight.

We lived in a children's camp near Harwich, England, and, from time to time, individuals would visit and select one or several children to take home with them. During these visits, David and I hid or made ourselves unobtrusive because we expected to be found by the relatives Father had promised to contact, and we didn't want to be separated.

About two months later, two cousins arrived, identified themselves and asked for us. Before the bureaucratic paper work was processed, I had been moved to an all-girls camp in Brighton. But they found me and I went with one, and David with the other. Our cousins lived in the same neighborhood in London so it was almost as if David and I were still together. We were happy to be with relatives, but tormented by the realization that we would probably never see our parents again.

In early 1939, with the protection of his Bolivian visa rapidly approaching its expiration date, my father decided not to wait for events to overtake him. He abandoned our home in Dresden and with Mother and Santo took a train to a small town near the Belgian border. There, for a large sum, he arranged for the three of them to be taken through a forest across the border. The small group set out late at night with the hired guide, and followed him silently through the woods, resting for a few minutes from time to time, until they crossed into the Belgian area of the forest. The guide wished them luck and disappeared back into the woods. My parents and brother were free!

They quickly made their way to Amsterdam and contacted an agency that could help them reunite with David and me. War clouds were darkening the horizon, and all European countries were starting to prepare for the inevitable. This slowed even the snail pace of bureaucracies, and children safely sheltered in England were not high on anyone's priority list. For five months, my parents remained in Amsterdam, unable to receive permission to pick us up in London, and waiting for the paperwork that would permit us to join them in Holland. Then events abruptly came to a head.

The Dutch authorities had initially informed my father that they would allow him to remain in their country only until transportation to Bolivia could be found. Suddenly, he was notified that the last ship scheduled for South America, a freighter with accommodations for only 12 passengers, was sailing in 8 days for Arica, a Chilean port near the Bolivian border. Would our family be ready to sail? If not, the five spaces would be assigned to someone else.

It was now or never. Father and Mother requested an immediate meeting with the elderly Dutch official in charge of the paperwork. During the past few months, they had gotten to know him as a warm and sympathetic person. He listened carefully to Father and recognized the urgency of the matter. Mother showed him my poem she had just received, in which I expressed my torment about being separated from my loved ones and wished that we would soon be reunited. I had poured out my heart and inner thoughts, and the official was moved. He leaned forward in his chair, looked straight into my mother's eyes, and said: "This matter is of an extraordinary nature, and I must take extraordinary measures. I will take your file to London and expedite the paperwork personally. We must not let this ship leave without you. Please stay near your telephone for the next few days." My parents were ecstatic. They firmly believed that their new friend would follow through.

And he did. A few days later, the official, whose name I never learned, brought David and me on the Channel boat to Amsterdam. He immediately called my parents, and our reunion was an outpouring of all the love, longing, despair, hope and anticipation that had been building up within us all these months. It was the happiest moment of my life.

We had three days to prepare for our journey. We bought clothes and various household items we might need in a strange land. Then we boarded the freighter and left the shores of a continent about to be consumed by war, brutality, and death. After several commercial stops along the way, the ship arrived in Arica, where we took a slow train to La Paz, Bolivia.

We lived with other refugees under primitive conditions for several months. I was overjoyed to find my cousins Gerda and Helga in La Paz. They had emigrated with their parents from Trieste months earlier, using the same $10 visa we had used. Eventually, we moved to a one-room "apartment." Father invested the $100 he had left in dry goods and peddled them door to door. With his business experience, he was successful, and life became easier for all of us.

We even adapted to the country's high altitude which had caused my mother and me much physical discomfort right from the start.

After almost three years in La Paz, Father moved his business to the tin mining area. Tin was in great demand all over the world, and the miners could afford the goods they needed. We settled in the village of Oruro, and there I married one of the refugees, a mining engineer from Berlin, and raised two children. The government honored the visa peddled illegally by its overseas employee for personal gain, and put no pressure on us to leave. We never encountered anti-Semitism or resentment. The Europeans started thriving enterprises all over the area and greatly enhanced the economy of that poverty-stricken nation.

In 1947, my parents sent the 17-year-old Santo to school in the United States. David followed in 1952. Both settled there and never returned to Bolivia. In 1954, the rest of us joined them and we were, once again, a close-knit family.

In Nazi Germany, Jews were willing to escape to any country, including some they could not locate on

Ruth Schwarz today

the map. Bolivia was such a place when, as a fluke, my father bought a visa for $10 from a greedy embassy employee in Trieste. Yet, it turned into the best investment he ever made. It paid its dividend in the survival of his entire family.

Four Fortunate Twists of Fate

As told by Israel Orzech

SOSNOVIEC, POLAND
HAIFA, ISRAEL

The First Twist

By the time I was 15, I was already a veteran of German slave labor camps. After five months in the grim Czech coal mines of Karvina in 1943, I was transferred to a construction unit at Markstaett, Germany, near the train tracks to Breslau. Both of my legs were breaking out in purulent sores, and the pus would often cling to my tattered clothes. The filth of the coal mine was taking its toll. Eventually, my foreman noticed my condition, and, because I was a good worker, sent me to the barracks for a week to recuperate. I had no medications, and healing was very slow.

On the last day of my convalescence, all sick inmates were ordered to report for a "special roll call." We all knew what that meant. Seventy to 80 emaciated and bedraggled men stood in an uneven line while an SS officer made the "selection." I was ordered to the left, to join about 50 others who were considered too ill to be useful. We were to leave the next morning for the Kosel extermination camp. It was my death warrant. There was no defense, no appeal, no reprieve.

We were kept in a large room at the clinic barracks to wait for a transport the next morning. The SS guards left. In the evening, Baruch Meister, the "Elder of the Jews" appointed by the Germans as overseer of all Jewish prisoners, and his Jewish deputy visited our group to say their goodbyes. For some reason, the Elder stopped in front of me, gave me a long but friendly look and asked: "Do you want to go to Kosel, young fellow?" "Sir," I replied weakly, "I can assure you I didn't volunteer." He smiled. "Where were you working, young man?" "Construction Unit Kaufmann," I said. "Then we can do something," he muttered. "They are short of workers and you look well enough to work." He told his deputy to take me back to my barracks. As we left, Mr. Meister called out: "Report to me tomorrow night after roll call."

I couldn't believe my luck. I would remain in Markstaett. At least for now, I would live!

The following evening, I reported to the Elder as ordered. He received me warmly and gave me an extra food card which would enable me to obtain additional rations for two months.

I wondered why he selected me. Did I remind him of a son or grandchild torn out of his life?

The Second Twist

The Markstaett labor camp was approximately three miles east of a huge factory complex built by prisoners for Krupp Industries. Approximately three miles west of the complex was a concentration camp, Fuenfteichen, which also supplied labor for the same factories.

In the fall of 1943, I was sent to a labor detail with the firm which maintained the roofs of the buildings and was preparing them for a harsh winter. It was backbreaking work, and the foremen were strict and ruthless. After four weeks, I was transferred to another contractor, Fuchs & Company, who was responsible for insulating the wiring in the central heating system that served the giant complex.

This new assignment was like a miracle. Cutting, packaging, and preparing insulation material was much easier labor. Since it was inside work, I was protected from the bitter winter and was also able to "appropriate" bits of materials and remnants which could be traded for food in the camp. But most important was the attitude and behavior of the Chief Supervisor Herbert. He was never harsh, cruel, or even demanding. His were the only kind smiles I had seen in years.

In January 1944, Labor Camp Markstaett was closed and all of its Jewish inmates were moved to Concentration Camp Fuenfteichen, on the other side of the complex.

The youngest prisoners were selected for kitchen duty. I was one of those fortunates. It meant indoor warmth, and all the food I needed. My hopes were high again. I would survive!

It lasted exactly one week. Someone bribed the

kitchen supervisor, a German inmate jailed for crimes, with gold coins and took my place. For a few days, I was bitter and depressed about this, but when I faced the realization that everyone was trying to survive by whatever means he could, I cast aside my disappointment and resolved that I too would survive.

I was transferred to a heavy construction unit. For ten hours a day, under constant pressure from overseers, I had to mix and carry cement. I was near physical collapse from undernourishment and fatigue.

One March day, while mixing cement, I felt someone's eyes upon me. I looked up and there was Chief Supervisor Herbert from Fuchs & Co., where I had worked three months earlier. He was obviously surprised to see me. "Hey little one," he exclaimed, "what are YOU doing in a construction gang? You look like you are not far from death." I told him about my short-lived kitchen job and how I was assigned to the work unit. He said that he had inquired about me when I failed to return to his shop following my transfer to Fuenfteichen. When he learned that I had been assigned to kitchen duty, he was happy for me and decided not to pursue the matter. "Little one, don't worry. You are coming back to me." With that he left. I didn't dare believe him.

Three days later, as my work group arrived at the factory complex, a loud voice rang out: "Number 25169, step forward!"

I was overcome with fright. I felt faint. Having your number called usually meant terrifying penalties or a death warrant. I stepped out of ranks and reported to the inmate-supervisor who had shouted the order. Near him, next to an SS officer, stood Chief Supervisor Herbert. He smiled. "Come, little one," he said, "you are coming back to ME." We walked to the shack that served as the Fuchs & Co. field office. "For the time being," he announced, "you will work in this shack and see to it that there is plenty of hot coffee and the stove never goes out."

I began to regain my health. Chief Supervisor Herbert would slip me sandwiches and other delicacies every time he visited the shack, almost daily. After a month, I was reassigned to my old job with the insulation materials and felt like a human being again.

The Third Twist

This feeling lasted until mid-January 1945. The Red Army was smashing its way westward and was rapidly approaching. The Fuenfteichen camps were disbanded and all inmates were forced to begin a six-day march through the snow to Gross Rosen Concentration Camp. Many died along the way. I barely made it.

Gross Rosen was jammed with prisoners from various eastern camps. A German prisoner named Nanke was the head of my barracks. On his shirt collar, he wore the green corner patch of those incarcerated for heinous or capital crimes. Because of the overcrowded conditions, we were fed our "lunch" of watery soup sometime after midnight. About two o'clock one morning, Nanke stormed into the stable that was our barracks. It was pitch black, and every inch of the floor was covered with sleeping bodies. Nanke carried a thick strip of lumber and as he screamed "up you swine," he swung the lumber right and left with all his might. Some people cried out in pain, and everyone scrambled to his feet to avoid Nanke's wrath. I wasn't lucky. A vicious swipe with the lumber found my right arm. I screamed in agony, but Nanke laughed. The pain was almost unbearable. I knew my arm was broken and it began to swell immediately. As soon as I could, I tried to control my anguish and to hide the arm and the pain. The alternative could be death.

A few days later, I was among those shipped to Buchenwald. Again, many died on the harsh journey. There were more inmates than there were tasks, so I rested and my arm started to heal. After a month, I was transferred to Concentration Camp Bissingen, near Stuttgart. There, "busy" work was created for us. We had to dig in mud gullies, without purpose or goal. It was to punish us. I tried digging with my left arm only, but my cruel SS guard thought I was shirking my work, and he beat me with a stick. I felt that he suspected something. Now I faced a dilemma.

If the guard discovered my broken arm, he would probably shoot me on the spot. If I asked for medical help, it could also mean my death. I decided to chance that rather than depend on the "good will" of the guard.

When I reported sick that evening, I was sent to a makeshift medical compound and faced an old Jewish-Hungarian doctor. He must have been over 70. I decided to entrust my life to him. I told him the story of my broken arm, the guard's suspicions, and begged him for help. "Young man," he said softly, "to help you means danger to my own life. But I'm old and you may yet survive. I can't treat you, but I will put you on the recovery list for the maximum time allowed, one week. Pray that you will feel better by then."

I was still on recovery status when all sick inmates were transferred to Allach, a smaller camp within the

Dachau Concentration Camp network. At last I was out of reach of the wrath of the vicious SS guard.

The Fourth Twist

By mid-April 1945, the German armies were in desperate flight on all fronts. The Soviets were approaching Berlin and Vienna on the eastern front, and the Americans were in hot pursuit of Nazi troops along the whole western front. I was on a train transport which was taking inmates to an unknown fate somewhere in the Austrian Alps. For several days, the train stood on the tracks south of Munich, awaiting clearance to proceed. It was heavily guarded by SS troops. Suddenly, an American combat unit, led by tanks and jeeps, surrounded the train and overcame the Nazi guards. They took them prisoner, and continued on. I walked in the direction of the American lines. In a small town named Tutzing I found a building where other liberated Jews slept and was shown to a bed. The next morning, I felt terrible and left to find medical help. I approached an American soldier and was about to speak when I collapsed. He took one look at my emaciated body, all 77 pounds of it, saw the fever burning my face, and called for an ambulance. After two days in the emergency area of a small hospital, I was shipped to a sanatorium near Munich.

Seven months later, one of the patients was overjoyed to receive a visit from his sister whom he had given up for lost. He introduced her to everyone around. We were happy for him, and a bit envious. The sister remarked that she had come from Sosnoviec in

Poland. For just an instant, I felt dizzy. That was my home town! "Did you know any of my family there?" I asked expectantly. I gave her the names and ages of my parents, four brothers and four sisters. "Yes, I met your sister Regina. She is alive and well in Sosnoviec." I broke into tears of joy, and relief. I was not alone. Someone in my family was still alive. There was no official mail service, so I directed a letter to the Polish Red Cross. I furnished the necessary details to find Regina and to advise her of my survival and whereabouts.

Two months later, in January 1946, as I sat in my room in the sanatorium reading a newspaper, my door slowly opened. I raised my eyes and there she stood. But it was not Regina! It was Nadia, my younger sister. Until that moment, I had no idea she was alive. We fell into each other's arms, crying and hugging. She had also been liberated from a concentration camp, returned to Sosnoviec and found Regina. As soon as the two heard of my survival, they resolved to come to me. It was not possible to leave Poland legally at that time, so each found a group that would take them out illegally. Nadia just arrived by way of Czechoslovakia. As we talked and brought each other up to date, the door opened again and in came Regina. Her train had just arrived by way of Germany. It was one of the happiest and yet one of the saddest days of my life. Before me stood the small segment of the family that survived. But they brought me the horrible details of my parents and brothers and sisters who did not.

We lived together in Munich until Regina met a fellow survivor, fell in love and got married. The couple moved to a town near Kassel, and Nadia and I visited her often.

Israel Orzech today

In June of 1949, Regina, her husband, infant son and Nadia emigrated to Israel. I missed them very much and followed in September. We lived near each other, raised families and kept the bonds tight and loving. Regina has passed on. At least she lived her final years in a safe and friendly environment. Israel became our refuge and haven, as it did, and still does, for Jews everywhere. That's why it too must survive—forever.

Unscheduled Stop

As told by Louise Lounah Abouaf Starr

PARIS, FRANCE
NICE, FRANCE

In 1492, Columbus sailed westward from Spain in search of a new route to spice-rich India. At the same time, when Queen Isabella signed the edict expelling from Spain all Jews who would not convert to Catholicism, the Abouaf family fled eastward. They settled in Smyrna, Turkey and lived there, in relative peace and comfort, in an ever-growing Jewish community, for 431 years. But in 1923, the area was embroiled in a Greek-Turkish war, as well as the Nationalist rebellion of Kemel Ataturk against the Sultanate. As a result, over 20,000 Jews fled to France, among them Moise Abouaf, my father, and his family.

We settled in Paris where my father started a small

142

knitting mill. He worked hard, expanded it, and added a clothing factory. He carried on the Abouaf tradition of success in business. We lived comfortably in the 11th District with many other Jews and also with Armenian Christians who had fled religious and ethnic persecution in Turkey.

Then the Nazi plague spread across Europe.

Calamity struck the Jews of Paris in July and August 1942. A Nazi dragnet swept up Jewish males wherever they were found. This was not difficult. The star with black letters "JUIF" on a yellow background that Jews had to wear helped in their quick identification and capture. My father and 17-year-old brother, Marcel, were arrested and shipped to Drancy Concentration Camp, a former police barracks on the outskirts of Paris.

It was known that Drancy, lacking extermination facilities, served as a transit point to the deadly installations in the East. No one remained there for long.

A family friend who was taken to Drancy reappeared in the city one day. He revealed confidentially that he had bribed some of the French and German camp officials with large sums, and they had released him. Two months later, my mother heard rumors that the Jews of Drancy would soon be shipped to death camps in Central Europe. We decided to go to Drancy to find some official we could bribe. Since our resources were very limited at that point, we sought the help of Mme. Raimbaud, one of my father's old business associates. Without hesitation, she gave my mother 100,000 gold Francs to help her rescue her husband and son. We felt it would be enough if we could only make a contact. If that failed, we thought we might at least catch a glimpse, however brief, of my beloved father and brother.

Very early one morning, Mother and I took the bus to Drancy. We covered our yellow stars with our pocketbooks. We looked like any middle-aged woman and her 23-year-old daughter on their way to purchase vegetables in the suburbs. We arrived at dawn and stopped in a small cafe, frequented by camp guards, where we hoped to make a contact. It was in vain. Although our yellow star was visible, nobody approached us or indicated any interest in us. After we gave up hope of finding someone to bribe, we walked silently but briskly for about ten minutes through the mist toward the concentration camp.

The camp was surrounded by a tall gruesome wall. There were several gates and sentry huts manned by armed military guards. Railroad tracks, part of the system that connected Paris to points north and northeast, passed close to the wall. The Germans probably selected that site for their camp because they could bring their military trains to its very gates. As we approached the tiny railroad station just outside the main gate, we were dumbfounded by the sights and sounds that unfurled. We took cover behind a small rain shelter about fifty feet from the station. We could see its three tracks clearly. On the track parallel to the main gate stood a locomotive with eight cattle cars attached. With horror in our hearts, we watched as Nazi guards pushed prisoners toward the cars. There were men of all ages, most wearing tattered clothes, some obviously sick, weak, lame, exhausted and barely able to stand. German rifle butts came down hard on anyone who didn't move fast enough toward the cars.

People were pushed into the compartment until it was literally stuffed to capacity. The sounds of anguish were unbearable. The Germans then closed the cattle cars and locked them with an iron bar on the outside.

The only openings were small air slits on the upper sides of the compartments.

Suddenly, from the cattle car closest to me, I noticed a face in one of the slits. Its eyes locked unto mine. Its lips moved. An emaciated hand, holding a piece of paper, appeared through the bars. The sight burned into my consciousness. "Un message, un message!" The man, probably standing on someone's shoulders, looked to me as his last hope to bring a message, or a goodbye, to someone he loved.

I reacted impulsively and rushed from my cover toward the tracks. The piece of paper had already fallen onto the ground and I felt I simply had to reach it. My mother lunged forward to grab me.

At that moment, a German Colonel spotted us. He was furious. He shouted an order for a guard to come after us. We began to run along the empty track nearest to us. We moved as fast as we could, holding hands, huffing and puffing. Suddenly, we heard a frightening sound of machinery approaching from the rear. With terror in our hearts, we turned.

On the tracks was a French train, made up of two passenger cars and about a dozen freight cars. It formed a barrier between us and the pursuing guard. The engineer vigorously motioned to us to come to him. As he came alongside, the train slowed and then stopped, but just long enough for us to jump aboard. The passengers who witnessed this rescue applauded. The train resumed speed, leaving the guard and his automatic rifle behind.

We expressed our gratitude, and the engineer introduced himself as Jean Louis Loiret, a member of the French resistance and a communist. He had surmised our predicament and was sure of his guess when he saw our yellow stars. Although he recognized the risk to himself and the other passengers, he was happy to make this unscheduled stop. He had often witnessed the brutal scene of wretched Jews being pushed into

Louise Starr today

cattle cars, destined for destruction. He was angry and sought vengeance.

As we neared Paris, he dropped us off at a freight depot. We took a bus home, returned the gold Francs we had been given, and tried to resume a semblance of "normal" life with my two younger brothers and my younger sister who was disabled from an earlier bout of polio. After five months, the situation for Jews became hopeless and we had to flee. We moved to the Parisian villa of my father's old friend, a Mr. Karayan. He was an Armenian Christian who had been saved as a baby by a Jewish family during the Turkish genocide of Armenians. Mr. Karayan had often told us to call on him if we ever needed help. He lived in an apartment in the suburbs and was happy to let us stay at his villa. Afraid to have the electricity turned on for a supposedly-empty house, he supplied us with oil and gas for cooking, tap water for drinking and bathing, and a 50-kilo sack of beans. He would visit us occasionally and bring us bread and vegetables. We remained hidden in Mr. Karayan's villa from April 1943 until liberation in August 1944.

We never saw our beloved Father and Marcel again. As Mother had suspected, they were shipped to Auschwitz and murdered. Our trip to Drancy was not only in vain but almost cost us our lives too.

A few weeks after our rescue at Drancy, we heard on the Nazi-controlled French radio that Cheminot (train engineer) Jean Louis Loiret was killed when, in a deliberate act of sabotage, he rammed his train into a German truck filled with explosives.

When the Allied forces entered Paris in September 1944, we went into the streets to greet our liberators.

It was exhilarating to be free again. We joined in the wild adulation showered upon the American and Free French soldiers by the happy people. I talked with many of the soldiers, but only one noticed my gold Hebrew medal. He gasped, "My God, you're a Jew! You survived! Tell me what happened." At last, somebody cared.

We moved away from the frenzy, leaned against the side of a building, and I told him my story. Visibly moved, tears streamed down the cheeks of this handsome Jewish sergeant, a combat veteran who had landed at Omaha Beach on D-Day. His name was Charles Starr. He served with a U.S. military intelligence unit, was an accomplished linguist, and a warm human being.

Charles remained in Paris, attached to S.H.A.P.E. Headquarters. We continued to see each other and, when he proposed, I "hitched my wagon to this Starr." Our wedding on December 17, 1944 was probably the first Jewish Franco-American marriage during the war. The honeymoon lasted only one day, but we made up for it. Together, we have brought forth a new branch of the Abouaf family, and, as in a fairy tale, we have lived happily ever after.

Desperate Search

From the memoirs of Harry Cohen
(1913–1982)

EDGWARE, ENGLAND

In early 1945, my British artillery battery was temporarily stationed in Sprang, a Dutch hamlet, to give the men and the guns a rest. Both had recently participated in the most intense artillery barrage the world had ever seen. It literally shook the earth on the enemy side of the Rhine and enabled the Canadians to hastily construct a pontoon bridge across that mighty river. This signalled the beginning of the end because it cleared the way to the Nazi heartland.

A cold drizzle, driven by intermittent gusts, passed over the area one evening when I had guard duty at the back entrance to our billets. My coat was buttoned high and my steel helmet was pulled down over my face, revealing only my eyes. I had been standing there for two deadly dull hours when the rhythm of rain and wind was broken by the feeble tinkling of a bell. A huge man on a bicycle, its wheels squelching along the muddy ground, came into view. His size made the bike look like a toy. He gave me a glance as he rode by and, a few seconds later, slammed on his brake, dismounted, propped the bike against a wall and strode vigorously toward me. Alarmed, I instinctively raised my rifle and assumed a challenging position. But that wasn't necessary. The man smiled, saying: "U bent een Jood" (You are a Jew). It was a statement, not a question. Completely taken aback I replied: "Yes, but how could you tell? You can barely see my face." "That's enough for me," he said. "To recognize a fellow Jew I only need to see his eyes." I smiled as we shook hands.

His name was Jakob, and he was anxious to talk. He told of his war experiences; that he had to leave his shoe factory and expensive home; and that a cobbler in Sprang agreed to hide him in a tiny cellar under his shop. Then he came to the point. "You British have plenty of things, and I haven't had tobacco for my pipe for the last four years. Can you give me some?" I promised to bring some to him the following day. He scribbled his address on a slip of paper, handed it to me and rode off.

When I found Jakob the next afternoon, he eagerly accepted the tin of tobacco and stuffed his pipe. He puffed aggressively on it, clouding the area in thick smoke. His conversation centered around the many items he could use. He hoped I would help him with his wish list. I was thoroughly uncomfortable and regretted having met him. I was delighted, therefore, when he offered to bring me to another Jewish family which had survived—and that is how I met the deJongs.

On a tidy, narrow street, we stopped at a drab, terraced house. In front, a tired-looking horse, hitched to a wagon, stood motionless, its foamy sweat still clinging to much of its hide. Jakob knocked on the door

Harry Cohen

and we entered. Inside, he introduced me to Mr. and Mrs. deJong. They were small, quiet, unassuming working-class people. They had light complexions and blond hair, which personified the "Aryan" look so treasured by the Germans.

Although we interrupted their sparse supper, they greeted us warmly. As Mrs. deJong served tea, they began to tell their story. She spoke a little English and translated for her husband who replied in German. Because I knew Yiddish, I was able to understand reasonably well. I was ready to listen, but the big man—he had heard it all before. Instead, Jakob began to babble away in Dutch to the deJongs. The more he spoke, the more embarrassed they became. Mrs. deJong blushed, and her husband vainly tried to stop the conversation, half-pointing in my direction to warn him that I might understand what was being said.

He was right. I had learned some of the language, and when my greedy "friend" referred to "tabak," I understood the sense of his conversation. He was obviously boasting about how he struck oil; a Jewish Tommy who was a soft touch and could become a valuable source of supply for tobacco and other goods. Mr. deJong looked at me and knew that I understood. He said something to the other man in sharp tones, and it brought immediate results—Jakob stood up, and without a word left in a huff. I was glad he had gone. I had completely lost interest in him and was anxious to learn more about the deJongs. They had a quiet but earnest air of stoic suffering about them and I wanted to know why.

We spoke in general terms about the last few years. They had decided to take advantage of their non-Jewish appearance and live openly with other Dutchmen during the Nazi occupation. They made a point of emphasizing that none of their neighbors betrayed them. This only reinforced my admiration for the Dutch people.

When I asked if they had children, they glanced at each other and seemed momentarily hesitant and uncomfortable. "Both children are asleep upstairs," Mrs. deJong began. "It's a pity you didn't come earlier. Jan is 7 and Rosie is 5." As if to end that line of conversation, Mr. deJong asked me to tell of my experiences since the Normandy landing. He leaned forward, listening with intense concentration to every word I spoke as if this would capture my feelings and in that way enhance his wife's translation. I told of battles, barrages, thrusts, and advances and brought my experiences up to date. I ended with "and now it's as good as over, and I am still alive." At that, the deJongs visibly tensed. Something was wrong. As if to prevent any inquiry, Mrs. deJong rose and said: "Meneer (Mr.) Cohen, please join us for Sabbath mid-day dinner."

When I returned on Saturday, Jan and Rosie were waiting expectantly to see "the British Tommy." Like their parents, they were fair-haired, light-skinned and without any Jewish features. I brought gifts for everyone—cigarettes for "Dad," a tin of canned corned beef for "Mum," and a large chocolate bar for each child. Mrs. deJong gratefully accepted the package for the adults, and Jan, taking his candy bar, bowed slightly to form an unspoken "thank you." But Rosie didn't reach for hers. She looked at me, then at the chocolate bar, and lowered her head shyly. Her mother laughed, picked her up to bring her face level with mine and said, "Go on, Sweetheart, take it. Meneer Cohen has brought you a nice present."

Rosie fingered the wrapping guardedly. Her mother, still laughing, removed the wrapper and silver foil. Rosie looked at the chocolate, touched it, lifted her face inquiringly toward both of us and asked, "What is that?" Her mother stopped laughing. I watched with fascination as the little girl savored her first nibble of the sweet ambrosia. Her blue eyes rolled and mirrored her pleasure as she irreversibly surrendered her taste buds to the newly discovered delicacy.

Mr. deJong was still out, so, after a while, we sat down for the Sabbath dinner without him. The dishes and silverware were artistically arranged on an immaculate table cloth. It was a reminder of better times. The meal, however, brought us back to reality. It began with a watery vegetable soup, followed by a serving of potatoes and vegetables grown in the family's small backyard garden, two cabbage leaves and three pieces of meat, each literally the size of a postage stamp. There was no dessert. Mrs. deJong confessed wistfully that she would have liked to surprise me with Oliebollen, a doughnut-like Dutch delicacy, if only she had the necessary ingredients.

After dinner, we sat on the horsehair sofa in the small parlour. I showed Mrs. deJong pictures of my wife and baby daughter, and, in response, she brought out her family album. Since film was not available to civilians during the war, most of the photos were several years old. Apparently, Rosie hadn't been born yet when these pictures were taken, and Jan was just a toddler, but on each photograph there was another girl. She looked like a 5-year-old, with jet black hair braided into a short pigtail. Her facial features were unmistakably Jewish, and her complexion was pleasingly decorated with a light sprinkling of freckles. A tiny smile curved her lips.

Who was this girl? I looked up at Mrs. deJong, afraid to voice the question in my eyes. She whispered, "That's my Betsy. She is nine years old now." Immense relief swept over me. Mrs. deJong had said "she is," not "she would have been." My whole body relaxed and so did the atmosphere. Mrs. deJong felt comfortable enough to bare her feelings, and told me the story.

When the Germans invaded, the deJongs were persuaded by friends and neighbors to hide Betsy in the countryside because she was so recognizably Jewish. Otherwise, it would be impossible for the family to blend with the local populace, and it could jeopardize everyone who helped them in any way. They managed to find a farmer in a remote area on the north side of the river Maas who was willing to take the great risk to shelter the little girl.

Mr. deJong frequently drove his horse and cart to the farm, ostensibly to buy food. He always passed near the barn where Betsy played with the farmer's flaxen-haired children. They would crowd around him and he would snatch a fleeting moment to pat his daughter's head and whisper a few words of endearment.

"I used to go and see her now and then myself," Mrs. deJong said, "but when we began to hear of the horrible things that were happening to Jews in Germany, we became afraid that our visits might be noticed and cause her to be betrayed, so we stopped going."

The successful invasion on D-Day brightened the deJongs' spirits. Their liberation and reunion with Betsy seemed imminent as the Allies surged forward through France, Belgium and Holland. But they met fierce resistance from the Germans at the last bridge at Arnhem, preventing them from crossing the river Maas. For six bitter-cold winter months, the liberating armies remained bogged down, unable to cross the river to the north. Throughout that gruelling winter, the deJongs were unable to establish any contact on the German-occupied side and their worry and concern about Betsy threw the family into consternation. Gloom pervaded the household. In the Spring of 1945, the Allies crossed the Maas on a pontoon bridge which miraculously supported the seemingly endless lines of military traffic crossing to the other side. Mr. deJong found the headquarters tent of the army authorities in the area. He explained that his little girl was at a farm on the other side and begged for permission to take his horse and wagon over the river. The officer in charge listened sympathetically but explained that it was not possible to permit civilian crossings until the main flow of military traffic was safely on the other side. Mr. deJong's frustration was unbearable. He appeared every morning to renew his plea. Once, even the Mayor came along to lend his prestige to the urgency of the request. After a week, the officer suddenly said: "O.K., you can go across. But you must report back here by sundown. Remember that!"

As he crossed the bridge, wedged between slow-moving convoys of tanks and lorries, his anxiety increased. How he longed to embrace and hold his little girl. He wished he could gallop his horse right through the damn vehicles and gain that extra minute with Betsy. As soon as he was clear of the bridge, he whipped his horse and dashed to the farm.

To his dismay, the farm no longer existed. It had been bombarded and burned to oblivion. Frantically,

Mr. deJong searched through the charred debris look-ing for a body, clothes, toys, or anything which might be identified. He found nothing.

Quickly he made his way to other farms in the area, but they also were destroyed and deserted. Dark-ness started to creep onto the horizon and he raced back to the bridge before it enveloped the area. The of-ficer in charge promised to allow another search the next day.

For two weeks, Mr. deJong was out from early morning until dark every day, travelling farther and farther afield, searching for anyone who could shed light on Betsy's whereabouts or fate. That is why Mr. deJong didn't join us for Sabbath dinner. He would be home at dusk.

What a courageous woman, I thought. Through-out the story, her voice remained soft and her smile was shy like that of a very young girl. I could imagine how she must have been feeling, and admired her in-credible control. I was very anxious to be there when Mr. deJong returned that night, so I napped on the sofa while his wife continued with her household chores. Later in the afternoon, we opened the tin of corned beef I had brought and had it for supper. When Jan and Rosie were ready for bed, they came in to say goodnight. They had gotten over their initial shyness with me, wished me "wel te rusten" (have a good night) and even kissed my cheek dutifully. It warmed me all over.

As daylight slowly evaporated, Mrs. deJong walked to the window every few minutes, peered through the curtains, her inner torment clearly im-printed on her face. When she saw the horse and wagon approaching, she quickly returned to the sofa and pretended to be in deep conversation with me.

He came in tired and haggard, politely wished us "goeden avend" (good evening) and walked toward the kitchen to wash. As he passed, his wife looked at him apprehensively. Almost imperceptibly, he shook his head.

For the next four weeks, his daily search continued. Sometimes, I was assigned to a duty near the foot of the bridge and I could see his horse and cart sandwiched between tanks and other vehicles. It looked pathetically bizarre. But Mr. deJong ignored occasional humorous remarks and serious comments. His eyes were always glued to the opposite bank of the river.

By this time, he had scoured the entire liberated territory, except for a small restricted area which was closed to civilians because of its strategic military link to the front lines. Each day, as Allied troops advanced, the restricted area shrank—and so did his hope of finding his daughter.

I was now deeply involved with the deJong family. Whenever I was off duty, I would hurry to their home to wait for the father's arrival in the evening. I no longer needed the slight shake of his head to know the despair. I saw it in his eyes every time.

Then came the shattering news—my artillery battery was ordered to Germany the following day. How could I leave without knowing whether the little girl was alive or dead?

With dragging feet and saddened heart, I made my way toward the deJong house. Deep in thought, I turned the corner into the street. The sight hit me like a sledgehammer! In front of the house was the horse and wagon. Several people stood at the front door, flowers in hand, and others were approaching, also carrying colorful bouquets. People congregating? Flowers? A funeral?

"Dear God," I thought, "let it not be so."

I raced to the house, pushed my way through the door and instantly, waves of relief rushed to my very core. The people in the hallway were laughing and drinking wine. Flowers were massed everywhere. Baskets of homegrown blooms filled the front windows, the front door, the hallway and all the steps on the staircase. I pushed through the people and flowers blocking my entry to the parlour I'd come to know so well and stood, for a moment, framed in the doorway, watching the jostling crowd.

In the center of the parlour stood Mrs. deJong and by her side was a little girl of about nine, with rosy cheeks, a few freckles, jet black hair plaited into a pigtail, and a face which was unmistakably Jewish. She tucked at her mother's sleeve and asked, "Who is that Tommy standing in the doorway?"

Mrs. deJong turned and saw me, took the child by the hand, walked over and, with a smile of elation, said quietly: "Meneer Cohen—this is Betsy. We found her on the last farm in the restricted zone!"

Motherlove

As told by Yolanda Grossman-Fischer Bernstein
(Deceased)

VRANOV, CZECHOSLOVAKIA
MIAMI BEACH, FLORIDA

Our family enjoyed all the comforts of the upper middle class, in our spacious home in Hrabovec, in western Czechoslovakia, near the Hungarian border. My father, Armin Grossman, operated a large stone quarry, employing over 800 men, and also served as a highway contractor, paving and repairing roads throughout the region. He was one of the few professional architects in the Czech provinces. He was also an orthodox Jew.

My mother died from a sudden illness in 1918, when I was only four. Father did his best to raise me, my older sister and brother, Etta and Bela, and my younger brother Layce. After two years, he remarried and fathered Hugo and Rosie. My stepmother Pearl brought us up as her own. We were a closely-knit family, and I always thought of her as "Mother."

My parents were thoughtful, considerate and generous people. For example, my father promised the principal of the town's Gymnasium (a secondary school preparatory to University) that he would grant scholarships to deserving medical students who needed financial support. It was Father's way of sharing his success with someone who was preparing himself to help others. During the late '20s and early '30s, at least eight young men were able to complete medical school in Bratislava because of my father's scholarships. The students would stop at the house to express their appreciation and report their progress whenever they could.

My mother, a woman of compassion, would often share our meals with our almost indigent next door neighbor, Mrs. Salasowichowa, who had suddenly been widowed and left with a young daughter, Maria. We looked after both for several years until the mother succumbed to a fatal disease. Maria decided to become a nun. She wrote us occasionally of her whereabouts and well-being and indicated that she was happy with her choice.

I married Isidor Fischer in 1935. As a wedding gift, my father built us a home near my husband's musical instrument shop in Vranov, in eastern Slovakia. A year later, my son Robert was born, and my daughter Marta arrived in 1938, three weeks before the Nazis marched into the Sudetenland, the western region of Czechoslovakia.

Hitler had inflamed German passions with a demand for reunification of the "persecuted" German-

Czech minority with the Fatherland, and Britain and France had sold out their trusting ally in the east, giving the Germans a free hand. They thought they had bought "peace in our time" with their treachery.

Encouraged by the weakness of the European powers, Hitler marched into the rest of the country only a few months later, in March 1939. The Czech Army was mobilized, and my husband kissed us goodbye and reported to his assigned unit. I took care of the children, ran the store and hoped for the best, not knowing that we would never be together again.

One morning a few weeks later, a Nazi officer entered the store, demanded the keys, and we were out of business. My father urged me to return to Hrabovec with the children since the Germans would soon requisition my house anyway. We joined him at his home on a large farm near the town. He still had many possessions, including his land, quarry, horses and wagons. But his most valuable asset was a special work permit from the Czech government certifying his occupation to be essential to the welfare of the state. It protected him against arrest or deportation with other Jews.

The Germans would often raid homes in the area, searching for hidden Jews, so the children and I slept in a barn most of the time. One night I dreamt of my departed mother. She warned that the Germans were coming and told me to go into the hills right away. The dream was so real that I awoke. In the distance, I heard a truck approaching. I grabbed the children and ran toward the edge of the farm and hid behind some poison ivy bushes, carefully avoiding its toxic leaves. The truck stopped at the barn, and Nazi soldiers

Yolanda with Marta and Robert

searched for us there and in the surrounding territory, but shunned the area near the bushes. When they left, we spent the night in the adjacent woods. My father found us, brought us food, and realized that he had to get us out of there.

The war and the occupation created new entrepreneurs, the risk-takers. They were willing, for a price, to defy the edicts of the authorities. They forged papers, hid Jews, smuggled goods and people, and took chances to make money. Father paid someone with a horse and wagon to take us to Kosici, in a Czech area which was annexed by the Hungarians when the Germans occupied the rest of the country. My husband's sister lived there and would surely help. At least we would be out of the clutches of the Nazis. Hungary was still independent, although sympathetic to Hitler.

We traveled at night and slept in barns during the day. We made it to Kosici and the guide left. My sister-in-law, Rose Lefkowitz, met me and we devised a plan. I would "abandon" the children and she would "find" them. As usual, the military authorities would turn the children over to the finder and they would be able to remain there legally with their aunt while I would go to Budapest, find a home and job, and then come back for them. The children had never met their aunt and would therefore not give the scheme away.

I sent Robert and Marta into a candy store and left the area. When they came back to the street, their mother was gone. They cried, clinging to each other, frightened and sobbing. Rose appeared from across the street, took them by the hand and walked them to the Kosici military headquarters. Much to her surprise and chagrin, they kept the youngsters and ordered her to go home. She notified me of this turn of events and I became frantic. "Go on to Budapest and leave the children," she advised. "They will probably be put in a home and will be all right. It will be easier for you to get along alone." But I would have none of this. I insisted on knowing where the children had been taken.

Following Rose's directions, I took a trolley to the end of the line. On a hilltop about a mile down the road stood a massive building, several stories high, which served as Hungarian Army headquarters. Guards milled around and when I approached, they stopped me. In the background, I saw my son and daughter playing with a group of other youngsters. I told the guards that I wanted to get my children back and they laughed. "Impossible," one of them said. "They are all orphans and are being shipped back to Czechoslovakia. We can't become baby sitters." As he and the other men laughed, I started to run toward the house. The guards swung their rifles at me and hit me several times, but I rushed on. The children saw me and came flying into my arms, and the soldiers beat us all. Annoyed at the commotion, the commanding officer appeared. He had me brought into his office. There, I revealed that I was a Jew and pleaded with him to let me take the children. "I have my orders to deliver them back to Czechoslovakia. We must hold you to verify your credentials." I cried and appealed to him. "Sir, you look like someone who has children of his own. You must know how I feel. Please don't separate me from them. At least, let me go with them." He thought for a long moment that seemed like an eternity. "All right, go with them, but they are leaving now." I thanked him, kissed his hand and ran outside where the soldiers were just lining the children up in formation for the long walk ahead. I took mine by the hand and lined up at the rear of the column. There were 35 youngsters and four soldier-escorts.

As we marched over the hill, my sister-in-law's son, Mickey, suddenly appeared on his bicycle, rode past the column at great speed, and dropped something at my feet. It was a small leather pouch, with a draw string to hold its contents. The Hungarian soldier at the rear of the column saw it and picked it up. I told him that although it was meant for me, I would like him to keep it. He untied the draw string and removed a handful of money. As he looked at me, I put an arm around each of my children, and smiled. He shrugged his shoulders and put the money in his pocket. About an hour later, as we came to a sharp turn in the road, the soldier quickened his pace and started to move forward from the rear of the column to the center, which was about to disappear beyond the curve. Without turning around, he waved his hand vigorously with a backward motion for me to drop out before reaching the bend. I grabbed my children and another boy who had walked with us and stepped off the trail, quietly lying behind some bushes until we could no longer hear the column. The little boy was an orphan and I felt it would be selfish to save only my own children when I had an opportunity to save him too.

For three weeks, we hid in the hills. During the day, I would lie on my back on the moist ground, the three children on top of me, covered with my coat to keep them warm. The dampness slowly invaded the joints of my body. My severe arthritis today is a constant and painful reminder of that time. At night, I would sneak into a village and beg for food. We wandered around and had to turn back when we reached a river we could not cross. I returned to Kosici to seek my sister-in-law's help and advice. I realized that I couldn't impose myself and three children on her. She told me that my father's special working permit had not saved him. He had been stripped of all his possessions and shipped to the ghetto at Sered. She suggested that I make my way to Budapest where I might find work and would stand a better chance to survive with small children. She even offered to buy the necessary train tickets for us. I saw no other alternative and gratefully accepted her offer.

In Budapest, I placed the children in a kindergarten and found work as a maid. I felt that life might become bearable again, but I was wrong. The Germans double-crossed their Hungarian allies and invaded the country in March 1944. They immediately herded any Jews they could find, including me, into a large petroleum plant near the city in hope that American bombers would spare the installation to spare the hostages. But the bombs fell and there were heavy casualties. I sustained many cuts and bruises and was forced to join other Jews in a column that was marched to the railway station where cattle cars stood by to take us to someplace called Auschwitz.

As the train got underway, I was hemmed into a corner of the cattle car, just below an opening that was spanned by several metal bars. My mind filled with the events that were overwhelming me. I had to presume that I had lost my beloved husband, and now my children were not with me. How and when would I get back to them? Why didn't I bolt from the column when they marched us to the train? How could I leave my little ones? I agonized and felt the despair in the depth of my soul. I grabbed the bars across the window, and the rotted wood around them crumbled and they came loose in my hands. On an impulse, I pulled myself up and jumped through the open space. I think I wanted to die.

The pain awakened me. I was in a Budapest hospital, my body covered with bruises and cuts, the scars from which are with me today. In my delirium, I must have called out for the children. The hospital staff found them and had them at my bedside when I came back to consciousness. It was one of the happiest moments of my life. Robert, showing the wear of a decade squeezed into his seven years of life, smiled and held the hand of his five-year-old sister Marta, to prevent her from jumping onto my shattered body.

I remained in the hospital about three weeks and during that time became friendly with another patient, a woman who was the manager of an apartment building nearby. She was a warm and sympathetic person and, when she was discharged, wished me well and expressed the hope that I would visit her sometime. She gave me her address and walking directions.

There was still a Jewish doctor on the staff. He came to me one afternoon and said quietly, "Mrs. Fischer, I must tell you that they won't hold you here any longer and I heard they will take you away tomorrow. I don't know where. Whatever you do, best of luck to you." I thanked him for the warning.

I had noticed that a large delivery truck pulled into the hospital yard every night at about 3 AM to deliver water and potato chips and to pick up empty containers. That, I figured, would be my way out. When the truck arrived, I pinned my nightgown between my legs, put on a coat, climbed out the window and hid behind a stack of empty water containers in the rear of the truck. My heart stood still when the men returned, dumped some more containers into the truck and drove away. When they stopped at a traffic light, I jumped off. It was 4:30 AM and I was in tremendous pain. I found my way to the apartment building of the kind lady I had met and knocked on her first-floor window. She looked through it with sleepy eyes but recognized me immediately. She took me in, fed me, and granted me the luxury of a bath. I had almost forgotten the feeling of peace that swept over me. The next morning, with warm clothes on my body and optimism in my heart, I went to the kindergarten, collected my two children, wished the little boy I had rescued the best of luck (he survived and lives with his family in Los Angeles), and started to walk north toward the Czech border. After about two weeks across fields and through forests, we came to a town which served as a stop for the train to Sered. We boarded it and made our way to my father in the ghetto.

It was an emotional and wonderful reunion. After a few days together, I left Robert with his grandfather and took Marta to Bratislava to seek medical help. The poor child was near starvation, and my body still ached from the jump off the train. I walked into a hospital with Marta, gave my name as Maria Wargowa, filled out a form and asked for help. The admissions nurse was adamant. "You can't just walk in here. You must have a doctor admit you," she lectured. "I will

call one of the house doctors and you can talk to him."
The physician arrived, glanced at the form I had completed, looked at me and invited me into a little room.
"Maria Wargowa," he said in low tones decorated
with a smile, "or is it Yolanda Grossman?" My heart
skipped a few beats. My forged papers proclaimed me
to be the Catholic Maria Wargowa. If he was about to
expose me, why did he smile? "Yolanda, you obviously don't remember me. I am one of the students
your father put through medical school. There are two
others here whom your father helped. Now, we can do
something for you in return. I will admit you and get
you and your little girl back on your feet. We will
cover for you as long as possible."

We remained in that hospital for about five weeks.
Those wonderful doctors saw to it that we had everything a person could need. They even notified my father that Maria Wargowa and her daughter were
under medical care and progressing satisfactorily. Our
bodies and souls began to heal. One day, I received a
postcard from my father, informing me that he and my
son Robert were leaving the ghetto the next morning,
destination unknown. Would I ever see them again?
Marta was all I had left.

When I felt strong enough to leave the hospital,
we said farewell to my three angels of mercy. I remembered that in her last letter, Maria Salasowo-
chowa, the neighbor's daughter who had become a
nun, had written that she worked in Sworadorf, a
Catholic home for college students in Bratislava. She
was delighted when I found her and invited us to stay
with her in her little room. She took care of us as best
she could, but after a week I realized I had to do some-

thing to earn money. Maria had little enough for herself to be able to share it. I decided to look for work under my adopted Czech name.

While walking the streets of Bratislava with Marta, a German contingent came out of nowhere and swooped up everyone who didn't have proper papers, including us. Trucks pulled up and everyone was taken to the railroad station, loaded into cattle cars and sent to Auschwitz. When we did not return, Maria must have understood our fate.

My job at the camp was to sort the clothes of the people who had been gassed, creating piles of blouses, trousers, shoes, and so on. It was late 1944, and my little girl, now six, worked with me at the gruesome task. I didn't know that my stepsister Rosie was in a barracks nearby, nor did I know then what had happened to my father and son.

The Germans liquidated the Sered ghetto and shipped its inmates to Theresienstadt Concentration Camp. They endured the harsh life, but with a measure of hope—they heard that the tide had turned against the Nazis. On Yom Kippur of 1944, my father, with Robert and 15 other men met secretly in a small room to conduct High Holyday services. The 8-year-old, tired and hungry, lay on the floor underneath the single bench, behind the legs of the men sitting above him. Over the melodic chant of the prayers, he could hear the sound of rain falling outside. Suddenly, the door burst open and several SS men stormed in. With sustained bursts from their automatic weapons, they mowed down the worshippers, who fell in a pool of blood where they had stood. The action took only a few seconds and the murderers left. The Jewish disposal crew would clean up in the morning.

Robert, unnoticed under the bench and hidden from sight by the bodies that had fallen in front of him, waited until the terror that paralyzed his mind subsided. He grabbed the body of his beloved grandfather by the belt and dragged him outside toward a dark area near a fence, leaving an undefined furrow in the mud. There, with his bare hands, the boy began to dig. He was only able to push aside the wet topsoil before he came to the end of his endurance. He ran back into the chamber of horror for a moment and returned to the fence. Slowly, with reverence, interrupted only by sighs of anguish, he spread a raincoat to cover as much of the body as he could. At least he could protect his grandpa from the rain. The next morning, Robert located my stepbrother Hugo in another section of Theresienstadt, and both mourned my dear father.

In May 1945, as the Red Army neared Theresienstadt, the Nazis ordered all remaining inmates into the mess hall. Hugo and Robert obeyed. When the huge room was full, a squad of SS men sprayed it with automatic rifle fire. People fell everywhere. Hugo dropped to the ground, pulling Robert with him. Bodies tumbled on top of them, enveloping them in a pool of blood. After the firing stopped, neither dared to move. They lay there, petrified and paralyzed for three days until they could hear the voices of Russian soldiers in the room.

Marta and I were liberated from Auschwitz by the Red Army, and we eventually made our way back to Vranov to see if anyone had survived. There, the au-

thorities informed me that they had word from
Bratislava that Robert and Hugo were alive and looking for me. We rushed back to the city and found
them, as well as Mother, Rosie and Layce, the "baby"
of the family. They were emaciated and weak, but
alive. It took several days before our tears of joy and
sadness ended.

The price of survival is heavy. Not a day goes by
that I don't think of my dear husband, father, sister
and brother who perished. My body aches and needs
constant medical attention. The physical and mental
scars are incurable. But it hurts less when I see my children and grandchildren, healthy and happy, or when I
hear from Rosie in Israel or Hugo in Australia. Mother
and Layce have gone to where the angels go, waiting
for the inevitable reunion with their loving family.

The Summons

As told by Morris Seidel

BERLIN, GERMANY
HALLANDALE, FLORIDA

When Adolf Hitler came to power in 1933, I lost my job driving a bus for the Municipality of Berlin. Jews were no longer welcome on the public payroll. Of course, I had to find other work to support my wife and young daughter.

The well-known firm of Furs by Julius Loeb hired me to drive its star salesman, a Mr. Katz, on his scheduled route to customers all over Germany. We spent four weeks on the road taking orders, and returned for two weeks to fill them. The next four weeks we again made deliveries and obtained new business. Since the panel truck carried valuable cargo, it had no markings to indicate its contents.

After visiting customers in the Munich area, Mr.

Katz always took a couple of days off in Switzerland. We had read about a good restaurant in the vicinity of Lake Constance, so we decided to eat there on our trip in June 1938. The restaurant lived up to its reputation. While we lingered after a delicious meal, I struck up a conversation with a Swiss businessman at the next table. He was easy to talk to and, during the conversation, I mentioned that I had been trying for two years to obtain a visa to anywhere so I and my family could leave Germany. The man leaned forward and told me quietly, "I can arrange with a friend in the Bolivian Embassy to get you a visa. It will cost you $500." To test the man's sincerity, I asked him for the name and address of the Bolivian official, which he gave me without hesitation. Then and there, I made the decision to take him up on his offer. I gave him my passport and the money (Mr. Katz lent me some) and we arranged to meet again on our next trip. This was a big gamble, of course, but in those times people took chances to get out of the country.

On our July break, he confirmed that everything was arranged. The Bolivian Embassy would send my passport and visa to the Jewish travel agency in Berlin officially designated to handle Jewish emigration. This would be done as soon as they received my written request. As was customary, I reported the pending Bolivian visa to the police when I returned.

The following month, after arriving in Munich and checking into the hotel, we were awakened at 6 AM and ordered into the street. Other sleepy-eyed people were already there. Adolf Hitler was expected to drive by at any moment and we served as the spontaneously enthusiastic and cheering crowd. Before

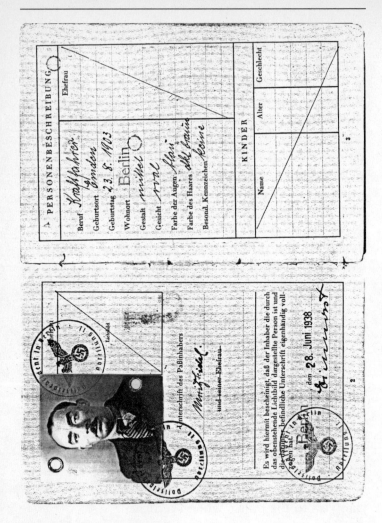

Morris Seidel's passport

long, he appeared, and Mr. Katz and I "heiled" him with loud, though faked, enthusiasm. The whole experience took only a few minutes, but we were now wide awake. Mr. Katz decided to use this available time to visit with a customer in Dachau, north of Munich.

I had heard that there was a labor camp for criminals near Dachau, but otherwise this was just another stop for me to make. The customer's store was on the edge of the town. I left Mr. Katz at the shop and parked in a clearing near a tree. I pulled out a newspaper, lit a cigarette, and relaxed. Had I looked straight ahead of me, I probably would have noticed the barbed wire fence surrounding many barracks and low-level structures.

Suddenly, I heard footsteps and voices. In my peripheral vision I saw an SS officer in his black uniform, and on the lower left sleeve the embroidered words LAGER-KOMMANDANT DACHAU (Camp Commander Dachau) in white. At the same time, I looked in front of me and realized that I was parked directly above the camp.

My mind put the two facts together, and it gripped me with fright. I fell into a dead faint. When I came to, the officer was gone. He had probably not even seen me. Mr. Katz returned, and we continued our trip.

Three weeks later, I received a letter at home. It ordered me to report to Gestapo Headquarters in Berlin on Alexanderplatz the following Monday, at 12 noon. A summons from the Gestapo promised unpleasantness, to say the least, and I planned to go alone. My wife insisted that she accompany me. "If something happens, it will happen to both of us," she argued.

On that fateful morning, we left little Rita with my parents and took a bus to Gestapo Headquarters. It was in an enormous building, occupying the whole block, with many entrances, each designated with a number. We entered through #2 as ordered. A uniformed guard looked at our letter and snarled, "To the fifth floor, lazy Jew-swine. And don't take the elevator. Walk it!" We climbed the stairs and arrived at the designated office, short of breath and tired. When I turned the door handle and took a step forward, a voice roared from within the room: "You goddamn Jews, when a German wants you at 12, he means 12. Now get the hell out of here and come back at the proper time." As I quickly closed the door, a clock somewhere was ringing its first of twelve slow chimes.

We stood in front of the office door and as we counted chime number four, a figure appeared down the hall and came toward us. He was a tall SS officer, in black uniform with silver and black collar patches attesting to high rank. He walked stiffly and barely gave us a glance as he passed us. Suddenly he stopped, turned, looked quizzically at my wife and asked cautiously, "Is that you, Elsa Bendit?" "Yes, Herr Minke," Elsa responded. "How are you?"

I had never heard this name and had no idea who this officer was. My wife later explained that he was a policeman in the Prussian town where Elsa was raised. He was a drinking buddy of Elsa's two older brothers. They spent many hours together in the local pub, telling jokes and chasing girls. At village social functions, Officer Minke would sometimes dance with young Elsa. "What are you doing here?" he inquired. Elsa showed him the letter. "Just a moment," he said as he entered the room we had hurriedly vacated just about eleven chimes ago. He returned with two chairs and asked us to take a seat and wait for him. After about ten minutes, he emerged with a file under his arm.

"You have been ordered here because the truck you were driving was observed in the area of labor camp Dachau last month, and they want to know what you were doing there. Look, I see that you have a visa pending to Bolivia, so I am going to take you out of here, for old times' sake. Just try not to call attention to yourself and keep a low profile. Now, follow me." He led us toward a fire stairwell at the end of the hallway, and we descended slowly. Meanwhile, Minke and Elsa chatted about her brothers and the good times the boys had together. We reached an underground passageway, followed it for a while, and emerged in an alleyway in back of the enormous building. SS Officer Minke extended his hand first to Elsa, wished her good luck, and then to me. With a twinkle in his eye, he advised me to take good care of her. Then he went back into the building.

We returned home, relieved by this fortunate twist of fate. For once, the German penchant for punctuality worked in our favor. But for the grace of four sounds of the chimes, we would have missed Herr Minke.

In mid-October, the travel agency notified me that there would be a boat leaving for Bolivia in December. I immediately wrote to the Bolivian Embassy official in Switzerland, requesting that the passport and visa be sent to the travel agency at his earliest convenience. He replied that the papers should arrive in Berlin by early November.

On the afternoon of November 9th, my employer notified me that the German Army had returned a

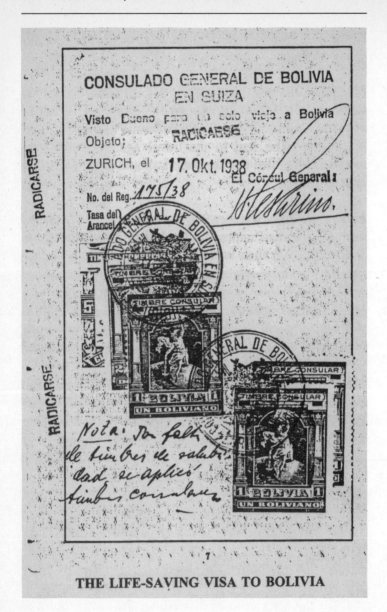

THE LIFE-SAVING VISA TO BOLIVIA

truck they had requisitioned a few weeks earlier for their invasion of Czechoslovakia. He asked me to come in ahead of time the next morning to drive the vehicle to a body shop where the military markings could be removed. In the early hours of November 10th, I drove the truck along Kurfuerstendam, the "5th Avenue of Berlin," and witnessed the havoc of the ignominious Kristallnacht. Police stood by while Nazi storm troopers looted and destroyed Jewish businesses, set synagogues afire, and brutally beat individual Jews caught on the streets. The crowds parted to let me through as I drove along. They respected the Nazi army insignia on my truck. On a hunch, I made my way to the Jewish travel agency. It was totally destroyed and on fire. My passport and visa were probably ashes by now. I was distraught.

When the pogrom died down, I returned home. In the next day's mail, there was a thick envelope from Switzerland. The Bolivians had made a mistake—instead of mailing my passport to the travel agency, they had mailed it to my home!

We left Germany legally and boarded the ship in Marseille. As we pulled away from shore, I thought I heard the resonant chimes of a clock slowly ringing twelve times.

The Escape

As told by Anne Andzia Bulka Potasnik (Deceased)

ZDUNSKA WOLA, POLAND
NORTH MIAMI BEACH, FLORIDA

Today, Zdunska Wola, approximately 25 miles southwest of Lodz, is a quiet Polish town of about 39,000 people, with no Jews. When I was born and raised there, Zdunska Wola was a thriving community of 65,000, of which about 40,000 were Jews.

My father had a small factory and supported us in comfort. Mother was the typical Jewish housewife, totally immersed in the well being of her family. In 1939, when the Germans marched into our city, I was a woman of 25, my younger brother Icek was in his teens, and my 32-year-old brother Jacob lived nearby with his wife. It was rumored that the Nazis were especially cruel to young Jewish boys, so my mother insisted that Icek make his way to the Russian part of Poland. This action saved his life.

At first, the occupation had no major impact on our lives. We greeted the same neighbors in the morning, went to work, and carried on our daily activities. By mid-1941, conditions changed. The Jews were ordered into the most rundown area of Zdunska Wola, a barbed wire fence was installed around it, and it became the ghetto. We lived there over a year. One night in the fall of 1942, the Nazis ordered all Jews out into the streets. They marched them toward a cemetery and directed families to stand together. Then they commanded the parents to step forward and loaded them on trucks and drove them away. It was the last time I saw my dear father and mother. They were taken to the extermination camp at Chelmno. The rest of us were transported in cattle cars to the ghetto in Lodz.

My brother Jacob, his wife Ruzia and I existed as best we could. I was a supervisor in a laundry, and they both worked in a blacksmith shop. In the winter of 1943, the SS rounded up everyone in our area and sent us to Auschwitz.

In the barracks, I was surprised to find two girls, Pola and Ester, whom I had known in Zdunska Wola. We became good friends. Joining us were two young women from Lodz, Mania and Sara. Since there was nothing to do, we talked much of the time, promising each other that, if one of us survived, she would tell our families of our fate.

After many months in Auschwitz, the five of us were part of a group of women shipped in cattle cars to Glogau, in Germany's East Silesia area. We were required to dig tank traps in the ground frozen almost

solid by the December cold of 1944. We were emaciated, almost skeletons, shivering under our scanty
rags, and hungry.

The young soldier in charge of our group divided
us into squads of five and appointed me supervisor
over my four friends. I would serve as lookout while
the others rested. When he came in sight, we would all
dig vigorously. One day soon after our arrival, he
called me over to the portable canteen that brought
food for the guards. I approached reluctantly. The
aroma was overwhelming to someone who had not
tasted anything palatable for two years. It made my
head swim and my mouth water. He handed me a
plate divided into three sections, one with soup, another with potatoes, and the third with meat. "Here,"
he said without any emotion, "bring back the plate
when you are done." I could not believe my luck. It
was manna from heaven. "Thank you, Herr Wachmeister [guard]," I stammered. Other soldiers witnessed the scene but showed no reaction. A few
inmates watched with envy but said nothing. The five
of us shared every morsel. It was a tremendous boost
to our morale. To our astonishment, this scene was re-
peated every day until the labor camp was dissolved
three months later.

I had open sores and wounds on my legs and
hands. The cold cut into them like a sharp knife. I was
in great pain and cried as I dug. The generous guard
noted my tears and asked, "Why are you crying?" I
explained my agony, and when I finished, he walked
off without further comment. After we returned to our
barracks, there was a loud yell. "Number 70,356
come here!" That was me. I walked in the direction of

the order and found my Wachmeister. He took me into a large store room containing piles of clothes collected from victims of concentration camps and ghettos all over Europe. He ordered a woman attendant to give me remnants to cover my hands and feet, a coat, and a cap. He walked off before I could thank him.

The Russians were smashing their way through the German lines along the whole front and the Nazis retreated, driving their slaves before them like cattle. Anyone who walked too slowly or fell exhausted was shot on the spot. Our column was thinning out. The five of us were toward the rear.

One day, I was not feeling well and had an acute case of diarrhea. I started to fall back and soon found myself next to the soldier who had been so kind to me. "Herr Wachmeister," I said, "I don't feel well and I can't walk much longer." As he slowed his pace to allow me to keep up with him, he replied without a hint of emotion, "So why are you walking?" I was puzzled. Was he implying that I had a choice? Was he giving me a warning not to continue on this death march? Did he slow down so I would not be shot as a straggler? I tried desperately to read his face but couldn't. My instincts told me he was hinting for me to get away while there was time.

This incident gave me new energy. I quickened my pace, caught up to the other girls and told them what had happened. "Tonight," I announced, "we are going to escape."

As evening approached, we were herded into a farm building, given some bread and soup, and everyone fell, exhausted, onto the concrete floor. At dawn, the five of us slowly rose and began to make our way toward a back door. The floor was covered wall-to-wall with people, and we could not avoid stepping on some of them. They woke up startled and cursed us. The commotion brought a blockleader, a Hungarian Jewess, to our side. She wanted to know what we were doing. I confided to her that we were planning to escape into the adjoining woods. She hesitated for a moment, embraced each of us and wished us success. She then held the back door open as we ducked low and ran into the bushes. The guards and their dogs

were asleep in another building. They were not worried about escapes. After all, there was nowhere to go and the cold would finish off any of the meagerly dressed, half starved inmates who tried it.

We walked deep into the woods until we reached a hill from which we could barely see the farm buildings we had left. Since we had no idea where we were, we decided to observe in which direction the column would head, and then go the opposite way. Promptly at 5 AM, we could hear the activities that began another day of the death march. We watched the column heading west, so we turned east and walked.

From time to time, we came to farmhouses or remote villages. We begged for food, claiming that our Polish employer deserted us and left us stranded without money, clothes and food. Our shaved heads were a sure giveaway that we were prisoners, so I made the initial approaches for food because I had a cap. If our benefactors realized the truth, they gave no indication of it, and helped anyway. One farmer's wife gave Pola, Ester, Mania and Sara head kerchiefs which gave them warmth and, more important, hid their nearly bald pates.

We walked for days. One late afternoon, we came across a barn with bales of hay neatly arranged in one corner. It looked so inviting, we decided to stay there and get at least one night of comfortable sleep. Unfortunately for us, the owner came by, saw five strangers asleep in his barn and called the authorities.

Two SS men brought us into the village. The officer in charge wanted to know where we came from and what we were doing there. I told him we all had lived in Lodz, gave a specific but false address, that our employer had deserted us, and we were on our way back to our home. He believed us. The officer rose from his desk and pointed out the window toward a large building on a hill. "That house is not occupied, so you can sleep there tonight and get on your way in the morning." We thanked him and our lucky stars and walked to the building. In one of the empty rooms, we huddled in a corner and fell asleep.

It must have been late morning when a noise awakened us. Our eyes took a few moments to get used to the bright sunlight that streamed through the window and embraced most of the room. Then we saw him. He was a short and bulky man and looked like a tough middle-aged Polish farmer. His biceps filled the sleeves of his polo shirt. I had seen his type many times and was afraid. I approached him, hugged him, and pleaded in Polish, "Please, Sir, don't take us back to the Germans." I thought by hugging him I could make him understand that we were human beings, with feelings just like his own. When he remarked, "Now listen to me," our fears increased. His was the obvious accent of a Ukrainian. They were known as zealous anti-Semites. Many of them welcomed the Nazis as liberators and served in a volunteer Ukrainian fascist division against the Russians. It seemed as if our luck had finally run out.

He must have seen the fear in our eyes. "Children," he began, "don't be afraid. I am hiding here with my wife and when you came, I had to find out if you were a danger to us. Come with me and you will be safe." With that he led us into a small basement. In one corner, the man pushed against the wall, revealing a five-foot-high opening on hinges. On the other side was a larger room containing a comfortable bed, a few wardrobes bulging with clothes, and food, lots of food. There were canned goods of all kinds, fruit, potatoes, and bread. We could not believe our eyes. The man's wife, a warm and friendly peasant woman, greeted us and invited us to eat. "Go easy on the food," our host suggested. "If you eat too much at first you will get sick. I have no medicines to help you." After we satisfied our gnawing hunger, the wife picked out some dresses for each of us and, as a crowning glory, pointed to a corner. Behind a sheet, we found a large basin next to a water outlet similar to that found in a garden. With immeasurable pleasure, we each washed our tired bodies deeply tarnished by misfortune and felt like a million Zlotys. What a wonderful feeling it was to sleep in a nightgown, even if the bed was a pile of straw.

The house had belonged to wealthy German sympathizers. As the Red Army approached, they fled in panic. The man and his wife had been forced laborers on a farm and took advantage of the confusion caused by the Russian advances to sneak off and find refuge in the large house. They brought what they could find upstairs down into the hidden storage room below that became their secret home. Their only view of the outside world came through a small window, probably meant for ventilation, which was parallel to the ground outside.

From time to time, I would peek out that window but could see nothing. About a week later, I heard noises, rushed to the window and saw the bottom of two boots. But they were not German! They were Russian! I turned to the others with a large grin on my face and announced, "The Russians are here. We are free!" My friends were exuberant, but the Ukrainians showed fear on their faces. The Russians might kill them because they were on the German side of the front. I quickly understood. "Please don't worry," I assured them, "The Russians will not harm us and I won't give you away."

A few minutes later, Red Army soldiers descended to the basement and we opened the hidden door and welcomed them with obvious pleasure. I spoke a little Russian and greeted them. "Ivraya (Jew)," I said. "We are Jews." I pointed to the girls. "No," the soldier in charge answered. "All Ivraya dead." "Look," I pleaded and ripped off my kerchief. The others did the same. The soldier's glance passed from one bald head to the other and he realized we were speaking the truth. His smile told me so. "And this nice Polish couple," I added, "helped us survive." Our hosts were standing there paralyzed. When the Russian soldier included them in his smiles, they relaxed.

These advance combat units were very kind and helpful to people not considered "the enemy." They took us girls to the village and selected an elegant German-owned home that had been deserted. They led us inside and told us to help ourselves to whatever we wanted. There were closets filled with warm clothes, shoes and hats, and I even found some American dollars under a large ashtray. A Russian soldier watched us with fascination, a smile wedged in the corners of his mouth. Suddenly he heard a noise in another room. Drawing his pistol, he ducked through the door. In the corner sat an old German in a wheelchair. His family had left him there when they fled. We heard a scream and a shot which silenced it. The soldier returned and continued his vigil. His smile never changed.

The soldiers who followed the combat units reacted to their surroundings from a different perspective. They saw survivors and liberated men and women in the fine clothes taken from the Germans, living in elegant homes deserted by them, and they classified them as bourgeois and stripped them of everything the combat troops had given them.

The five of us decided to go back to our home towns and started the long walk. Once, someone gave us a ride on a horse-drawn cart, and we stayed with him as he went from city to city toward his final destination until, one day, a Red Army patrol stopped him and took his horse and wagon. After a few weeks, Mania and Sara left us to proceed to Lodz, and I continued with Pola and Ester to Zdunska Wola.

We arrived there in the early evening, unaware that a 6 PM curfew was in effect. We were frightened and surprised when Polish police stopped us and brought us to their station. We explained our circumstances and their attitude changed instantly. They escorted us to a large house from which the German owners had been ousted and which now served as a temporary shelter for Jewish survivors. Pola and Ester went their separate ways, and I registered with the authorities and asked if they knew if anyone in my family had survived. They did not. I returned to the house in which I was born and raised. The Polish family living there reluctantly heard my story and gave me some food and a few Zlotys. They were relieved when I left. I was too sick, lonely and sad to care. When I walked the streets of my old neighborhood, several people recognized me. I was shocked when one of them exclaimed, "You are still alive? I thought they finished you off once and for all." I felt dizzy. This was my homecoming?

I sought out my old doctor. He was still in practice and welcomed me warmly. He inquired about the rest of my family and was genuinely sad to hear that no one had survived. He checked me into a hospital and I remained there until I had regained my strength and my hair.

Because a cousin in Lodz had registered with the authorities, I learned that he had survived the concentration camps. I visited with him for three weeks. It was there that I met Herman Potasnik, a kind, gentle man who had known my parents in Zdunska Wolla. He proposed marriage and promised a new peaceful life.

The ceremony took place in Lodz, under a Chupa (canopy) made of a patched sheet. It was performed by an old rabbinic-looking Jew, his scraggly beard starting to cover his slender face. No one asked to see his credentials. His prayers and blessings rose to the heavens with clarity and pride.

An uncle in America provided us with an affidavit and we settled in Massachusetts. Members of the Jewish community in Lynn co-signed a note that allowed us to open a small grocery store. We worked hard, repaid the loan and resumed a normal life. Our greatest pride came the day that our only son, Joseph, was ordained as an orthodox Rabbi. For us, this was not only a personal joy, but it reaffirmed that Hitler did not win—Am Yisroel Chai! The People of Israel Live.

On the Train to Survival

As told by Anna Lautman

TLUMACZ, POLAND
MIAMI BEACH, FLORIDA

The little village of Tlumacz, near Stanislaw, Poland, was our home for generations. Most of the 5,000 inhabitants were orthodox Jews. My father sold fish and fruit he bought from the Ukrainians near the river and in the countryside. He was able to provide a comfortable life for his wife and nine children. I was the second youngest at 17, when the Germans and Russians divided Poland in 1939. We lived on the Russian side of the Bug River and carried on our daily lives as best we could.

In late June of 1941, we heard that the Nazis would soon attack. When bombs began to fall, a group of village youngsters organized to evacuate to the countryside where they would dig trenches and shelters to hide from the Germans. I wanted to join this group. My parents reluctantly gave me permission but turned a deaf ear to my plea to come with me. They didn't want to leave their home and possessions.

Our horse-drawn wagons had barely reached the countryside when Nazi planes roared out of the clouds and bombed and strafed us for several minutes. The horses and many of the youngsters were killed or wounded. I joined others running eastward in panic.

We came to a small village railroad station where a train was about to leave, and we jumped on and squeezed ourselves into one of the overcrowded compartments. It was pure hell. There was no food, water, or facilities except when the train stopped. Then, some people would leave and others would squeeze on. I had nowhere to go, so I stayed on the train. Three days later it reached its destination, Kiev in the Ukraine.

I wandered around the vicinity of the railway station like a lost sheep. I walked through a small farmers' market where a woman took pity and gave me some food. Although I was 17, I was so emaciated that she thought I was a child and took me to a kindergarten where other small children stayed.

I regained my strength and began to feel like a human being again. I asked to be given some work and was sent into the hills to pick vegetables and fruits. Later, I was transferred to kitchen duties in a sugar factory, where I had a place to sleep and something to eat. But this sudden comfort was short-lived. About three weeks later, everyone began to run—the Germans were coming!

A fire engine, revving its motor furiously, was about

to leave, so I and several others jumped on its running boards and held on for dear life. The vehicle sped eastward, its engine roaring as it cut through the clouds of dust stirred up by its tires. At night, we stopped at a village. I went from house to house seeking food and shelter. At one tiny hut, a woman who had fled from Minsk with her two small children gave me a piece of bread and invited me to share the bare floor with them. My exhaustion overcame the discomfort and I soon fell into a deep, refreshing sleep. After two nights, the kind woman said to me, "Anna, I can't go anywhere. I have to stay to find food for my children. But you are alone and shouldn't be here when the Germans arrive. There is a railroad station just a few miles away and they have a Russian Red Cross unit which takes care of the military hospital trains that stop once in a while. I'm sure they will give you food and shelter." I took her advice, thanked her for her kindness and left.

As I arrived at the station, a train full of Russian soldiers was pulling in for refueling. I stood on the platform watching with great interest, when a uniformed lady with the rank of a medical officer engaged me in conversation. "Little girl, are you with your mother and father?" she asked. "No," I responded, "I am all alone." "Where are you going?" she continued. "I don't know. I am running away from the Germans," I said. She looked at me with warmth and compassion. "Little girl," she began "I will take you on the train with me and tell them you are my assistant nurse. Don't say or do anything that can get me into trouble." I was grateful. She took me to her compartment on the train, left me to go to a nearby market and returned with bread and jam.

The train pulled out after an hour, and I relaxed in

my new home. I felt safe again. For over a week, I cleaned compartments, washed floors, helped feed the troops, and performed whatever duties my lady doctor requested. These soldiers were on their way to Stalingrad to defend that city. I was the only civilian on the train.

When we arrived near Stalingrad, the soldiers disembarked and marched off. My benefactor wished me well. I thanked her sincerely, and we said our goodbyes. What would I do now, I wondered?

I looked around and, at the other end of the station, saw a military hospital train full of wounded soldiers. I learned later that this train traveled just behind the fighting lines, picked up wounded soldiers and brought them to hospitals in the interior. I approached a soldier and asked to speak to the commanding officer. After several referrals from one person to the other, I eventually was led to a handsome, tall man whose uniform indicated an officer of high rank. Although he seemed very busy, he listened attentively. I told him how experienced I was with work on trains— after all, I had just completed over a week on a troop train—and asked him for work. He smiled and apparently took a liking to me. He pointed toward a pretty, well-proportioned woman in a white uniform. "Tell Lucy, the Head Nurse, that I sent you. She will give you a job." Then he added, "She's Jewish."

Lucy, who was the commander's girlfriend, was glad to have me. She gave me a white nurse's uniform and introduced me to a few others girls who had joined the staff. During the day we worked on the train, and for several evenings attended classes on how to become effective nurses. I had enough to eat, a place to sleep, nice people to work with, and I felt useful. My life had purpose. But one theme constantly gnawed at my thoughts. What had happened to my family? There were many military casualties, and we worked hard to comfort, feed, wash, and talk with the weary combat soldiers. This train was my home for almost three years.

In mid-1943, the Germans had been defeated at Stalingrad, and the Red Army was in hot pursuit along the entire front.

On one occasion, we were transporting the wounded to hospitals in Rostov. It was a long train with approximately 60 cars, each holding about 30 patients. I was on the night shift with 19 other girls. It was exhausting work, with never a moment's rest. At 8 AM, we arrived in the Rostov railroad yards, just as the night shift ended.

The night nurses rushed off to the forward car, which served as our quarters, and collapsed into their bunks from fatigue. Although I was also dead tired, I decided to stay and help the day shift serve breakfast to the wounded who could not feed themselves and would have had to wait until the others were served. I had done this before, and the day nurses and patients really appreciated it. I would get to sleep an hour later.

While the other nurses went to the kitchen car to get the food, one nurse remained with me in the compartment to prepare the men for breakfast. Suddenly, a piercing sound broke the usual din of voices and activities. I had heard it before. A Nazi Stuka dive bomber broke through the clouds and dropped a bomb on the train even though it was clearly marked with large red crosses on the top of each car. Death landed squarely on the nurses' quarters, blowing my 19 co-workers on the night shift to oblivion. When I realized I would normally have been there, I began to shake. I was frantic—the train was a sitting duck.

I rushed to the entry steps of the car and saw a supervisor running by. I screamed at him: "What

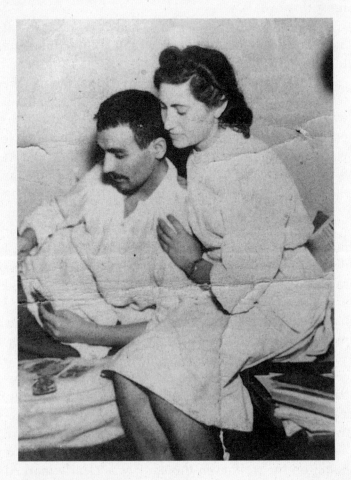

Anna nursing Russian soldier

should I do with the patients?" "Just leave everything as is. Do nothing," he ordered and ran on. The other nurse and the soldiers in the car looked terrified. I just couldn't see letting 30 men lie there helplessly, awaiting death. I decided to do something, orders or no orders.

There were about a dozen civilians standing on a small covered platform near the train. They were staring at the burning remains of the nurses' car. I leaned out the window and screamed at them to come help take the wounded out. They rushed forward. The other nurse and I carried or led one man at a time toward the entrance, and the civilians took them off the train and laid them under cover of the station, behind trees, anywhere that could provide shelter. Just as we carried the last patient off the car, we heard the ominous piercing sound of the Stuka again. He plunged out of the clouds and, within seconds, the car we had just left blew to smithereens, wounding several people with flying fragments. The Nazi plane returned once more, strafed the train, hitting many, and disappeared into the clouds, its ammunition spent and its mission of death accomplished. When trucks arrived to take the wounded to hospitals, I noticed that the supervisor was among them, his face covered with blood. Surely he would not charge me with disobeying his orders now. He had his own problems.

The fighting was so fierce and the Germans so ruthless in their desperate bid to stave off defeat that the hospital trains were discontinued. I remained in Rostov, and as the Red Army pushed westward, I was assigned to various field hospitals. Eventually, the Germans were completely cleared out of the Soviet Union, and our forces entered Poland.

I was assigned to a field hospital in Poznan, and one night, the sky suddenly turned bright with light from flares and explosives. The noise was deafening and the ground trembled. Were the Germans counter-attacking? Someone screamed: "Anna, it's over! The war is over!" People hugged each other and danced with joy.

The next morning, I reported to the hospital commander and begged him for papers to enable me to return to my hometown and see if anyone of my family had survived. He was sympathetic but advised me not to go back. "All the Jews in that area were sent to con-

Anna today

centration camps. There is no one left. If you go back, the Ukrainians will kill you on the spot." I took his advice. Later, a distant cousin who was hidden by a Gentile friend confirmed the commander's suspicions. Every member of my family had perished.

To this day, I sometimes dream of the railway station in Rostov, the Stuka dive bomber, and what might have been. Then I think of the soldiers we pulled out to safety and I am able to sleep peacefully again. They were lucky that I was lucky.

Flight from Peril

As told by Benno Elkus

DENEKAMP, HOLLAND
MELBOURNE, AUSTRALIA

We lived with apprehension as news reached us of repressive measures taken against our fellow Jews in Germany. Our lives in Holland had been pleasant and routine for generations. Our small village of Denekamp was only a few miles from the German border. There was nothing we could do about the events in Germany except hope that its evil would not expand to our neutral nation.

My father, a warm, loving man, was a cattle merchant and meat exporter. He provided well for his wife, two daughters and three sons.

In 1939, I was a strapping youth of 24 and worked as an assistant manager of a leading Dutch textile firm's branch in Enschede, about ten miles

204

south of our village. I also dabbled in art. When the Germans invaded Poland in September, I was drafted into the Dutch Army. After the fall of Holland in 1940, I was discharged and returned to my job in Enschede. From then on, everything went downhill.

The Germans took over the textile plant from its owners and discharged employees discovered to be Jewish. Because I was management, I was the last to be fired. Back in Denekamp, a friendly clogmaker named Bernard Lubberink allowed me to work in his shop. He created a variety of the popular Dutch wooden shoes. A few weeks later, a Dutch Nazi arrested me, claiming I had defaced the sidewalk with a large W, the initial of the exiled Queen Wilhelmina. I was locked up at the local police station. Mr. Knippers, the owner of an artists supply shop, sent me paints, brushes and canvas. The anti-Nazi Dutch police at the station permitted the supplies to reach me. Meanwhile, friends and colleagues, Dutchmen who knew me in my village and in Enschede, intervened with the authorities and pleaded my innocence. Six weeks later, the SS commander at Enschede authorized my release.

Fearing more unjustified arrests, I fled to the south where Jewish friends found a farmer willing to hide me. But a local Nazi became suspicious, and one of the farmers sent me a message that questions were being asked and urged me to leave immediately. I bicycled to my parent's home in Denekamp. There I learned that my older brother, Lutze, had been seized and a telegram had arrived stating that he had died of "pneumonia" in Mauthausen Concentration Camp in

Austria. A dark cloud of sorrow swept over us. There was a feeling of impending doom for us all.

By this time, Jews had to wear yellow stars, could not associate with Aryans and had to surrender their radios, cars, motorcycles and bicycles. In mid-1942, a letter arrived, ordering me and my "baby" brother Jacob, seven years younger than I, to report to the bus station for transfer to the labor camp in Zutphen, about 45 miles west. The friendly clogmaker advised us to hide, but we felt it had become too risky for any-one to help a Jew. With heavy heart we bade our family farewell, promising to stay in touch if possible, and hoping for an early reunion. I had the foreboding it would be a long time before we were together again. Little did we know that my parents and sisters all would perish in Auschwitz only a few months later.

At the labor camp, most inmates were forced to dig drainage ditches. I was assigned to look after the sick and feeble. All I could do was comfort them and try to keep their courage alive. A barbed wire fence surrounded the camp. But it was thin wire, and from time to time Mr. Lubberink, the clogmaker, would push small parcels of cheese or bread through by bending the wire upward at ground level.

Two months after our arrival, on a misty Saturday morning in October 1942, the camp commander an-nounced that all prisoners would be transported to Westerbork Concentration Camp, a well-known Dutch transfer point to Auschwitz. The inmates were in a panic. Jacob insisted that we take the initiative and flee. I agreed and followed him as he crawled to-ward the fence, miraculously escaping detection, and crept behind him through the fence. We ran across a field of grass and found cover behind some bushes.

Fearfully, we made our way through a nearby village. Our tattered civilian clothes and frightened movements were clearly suspicious, but no one gave us away. We found some raw grain that must have leaked from a farmer's sack and ate it. Some of the 10-gallon milk cans, customarily left at roadside for collection by the dairy, contained leftover milk which we drank. A baker boy making deliveries gave us a loaf of bread. We decided to make our way to Enschede where we had friends.

We carried some money and razor blades we had hidden while in the labor camp. We cut away the yellow stars from our clothes, painfully shaved our faces without soap or water and, at the next town, bought train tickets. We had no papers whatsoever. At the station, we kept our faces down and turned toward the window while on the train. Although there were German soldiers and SS everywhere, no one challenged us. We made it to Enschede.

Our sister Leni had known Toos Van Tol since childhood. The girls had played together, learned together and continued their friendship after Toos was married. Their dissimilar religious beliefs never affected their relationship. Now Jacob and I rang her front door bell, seeking refuge. She welcomed us cheerfully and invited us in. When she heard our experiences, she insisted we stay in an upstairs room of the house. Toos and her husband, Albert, were totally unafraid. When 5-year-old Edward and 2-year-old Ronald noticed their mother carrying food up the stairs, they were told that Santa Claus and his faithful servant Black Peter, characters revered by Dutch children, were resting there. As any child would, little Edward proudly bragged to his playmates that Santa Claus was staying in his home.

It was difficult for Toos to feed two additional people on the meager rations to which she was entitled. She appealed for help to Pastor Overduin, well known in the area for aiding Jews and underground members. He provided her with additional food coupons and visited us to encourage us to survive.

During the next six months, we lived undisturbed and developed a false sense of security. At night, with the children sound asleep, we would come down, have coffee and visit with Toos and Albert. We didn't even

Edward, Toos, Robert

bother to keep our voices low. Anyone walking past the house on the nearby sidewalk could hear that more than two people were socializing late at night.

One Saturday afternoon in October 1943, we heard three tolls of the front door bell. Albert had sounded our prearranged alarm signal. I alerted Jacob, who was reading, and I slowly began to descend the stairs to find out what was going on. Through the doorway leading to the sitting room, I saw Albert staring ahead into the area near the front door which was not visible to me. A Dutch detective, well-known as a Nazi collaborator, had arrived to investigate a lead. When he noticed Albert's eyes moving in my direction, he darted through the room and headed toward me. I screamed in terror. As he grabbed my arm, I shoved him with all the strength I could muster and he fell backward, down the stairs. My brother had already stepped onto the roof through a door adjacent to our room, and when I reached the top of the stairs I joined him. We ran to the edge, jumped to the ground, landed near a group of playing children and ran. We crossed many backyards, gardens and fields until, exhausted, we reached the outskirts of the town and collapsed in a potato field. During the next several days, we slept in ditches and hid in occupied and vacant barns. Often, we heard police searching for us with their dogs and feared the worst. But we were not discovered.

We decided to seek help from Farmer Holskorte, an old family friend who had spent many hours by the stove in our dining room exchanging yarns with my father. He lived just outside of Denekamp with his unmarried sister and his 40-year-old adopted bachelor son, Geit, also a friend of our family. We walked at night to reach the farm, about 12 miles away. We were greeted warmly, fed and housed. Farmer Holskorte was apprehensive. "If they discover us, the Germans will kill us all." But Geit was not afraid. He insisted that we remain with them. He had a plan.

About 100 yards from the house was a large empty barn, now serving as a storage room and pigsty. There was a space underneath it, approximately 40 inches high and 8 feet wide and extending the full length of the barn. This had been a manure cellar. Outside the rear wall was an opening on the ground, covered by a concrete lid, through which the manure could be poured into the cellar. Within the barn near a window at the front wall there was an entrance through a small trap door that led to the other end of the manure cellar below it. The walls were made of brick and plaster. Although the cellar was clean, the high Dutch water table kept the floor under several inches of water most of the time.

During the next four days, while we hid in a hay loft, Geit scooped out the water by hand until the floor was relatively dry. He then built a brick wall, about 15 inches high, across the width, creating a small room underneath the trap door at the front end of the barn. Anyone looking down into the cellar at the outside entrance in the rear would only see water. Because some moisture would still seep through the dividing wall, Geit laid bricks on the ground, bridged them with wooden planks, and topped these with straw.

Two woolen blankets and clogs helped us keep our bodies warm and our feet dry. We never changed clothes and only occasionally ventured out of our dark

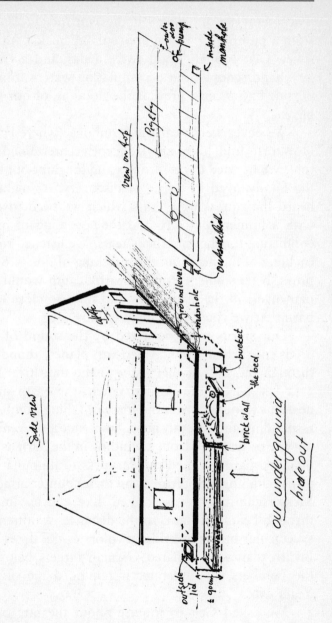

Our underground hide out

world to wash our naked bodies with icy cold water from a pump in the barn above us. A bucket was our toilet. Geit brought food twice a day and a trusted farmhand scooped out accumulating waters from the outside entrance to prevent the flooding of our small haven.

We never went near the farmhouse where Farmer Holskorte and his sister frequently entertained visitors. We listened to their toasts and laughter but knew the family lived in terror of discovery. At night, we heard the squeaking of rats which we tried to catch with a homemade trap, and the squealing of piglets competing for their mother's teats. We listened for the cackling of the hens and the quacking of ducks. Sometimes, Nazi soldiers from a nearby camp would hold maneuvers in the farm areas and were so close to the barn that we could hear them talking.

Our spirits were bolstered by the sound of hundreds of British and American planes thundering through the sky on their way to the industrial Ruhr area just across the border. Often, the earth underneath us trembled from the force of falling bombs and responding anti-aircraft guns. Sometimes, we ventured outside or watched from a window in the barn as German spotlights slashed the darkness to illuminate approaching English Spitfires and their counter-attacking Messerschmitts. They looked like moths lunging through beams of light. In the distance, we often saw spectacular bursts of brilliant colors as the flares from British planes illuminated German targets below for the bombers to obliterate. It reminded me of New Years Eve.

We asked Geit to inquire about the fate of our

family. He reported that all Jews had been rounded up on Wednesday, November 18, 1942 and transported to Westerbork, the transit point to Auschwitz. From that day, Jacob and I fasted every Wednesday, in honor and memory of our loved ones.

Most of the time, unable to stand erect in our close quarters, we lay on our straw bunk, occupied with our thoughts. Mine were mainly religious, emphasizing a trust in God and an awareness of his presence. I doubt that Jacob shared these feelings. He was less of a dreamer, more assertive and down to earth. He had led me across the roof out of the Van Tol house, initiated the escape from the labor camp and found refuge with Farmer Holskorte. Without him, I probably would not have survived. Often, I fantasized about the beautiful scenes I would paint when we were rescued. I catalogued these ideas in my mind.

In the winter of 1944, I thought I would lose Jacob. He suddenly became very ill. Geit told us there was an epidemic of influenza in the area. It somehow must have reached our underground hiding place. To escape the dampness, we left our cellar and climbed to the loft packed with hay. Jacob had severe diarrhea and discharged blood. Farmer Holskorte and Geit became very concerned about the possibility of having to account for the presence of a deceased person on their property. A doctor was, of course, out of the question. I cared for Jacob as best I could, prayed for his recovery and prepared myself for the worst. As suddenly as he had become ill, he recovered. We were overjoyed. We returned to our underground haven.

On May 4, 1945, we were alarmed and then surprised to hear Geit running toward the barn, shouting our names. It all became clear as he exclaimed, "Boys, come out! We are free!" The British Tommies had just liberated the area. We emerged from the darkness that had enveloped us for almost two years into an unreal world of light and laughter. Arm in arm with others, we marched into Denekamp, reprieved from the misery of the past, yet deeply depressed that only we had survived.

Then we learned that my former colleagues at the textile works, after discovering where we were hidden, had arranged with the Dutch administrator of the factory to fake the books and continue my salary. The money was sent by courier to Farmer Holskorte to pay for our upkeep. This was done behind the back of the German trustee appointed to oversee the operation.

We further learned of the events that followed our escape from the Van Tol home. Albert avoided immediate arrest by convincing the Dutch collaborator that he knew where we could be located and that he would deliver us personally. Instead, he fled into hiding. Unfortunately, he was caught and locked up in the prison at Utrecht. Albert's sister had for years worked at the very prison as an officer and had often supplied the Underground with information about important inmates. With her brother's life at stake, she maneuvered an escape and joined him in hiding.

Albert's wife Toos, unperturbed by these events, took three more Jews into her home. They were discovered and Toos was given the choice of losing her children and being sent to a concentration camp for extermination or keeping her children and serving Nazi soldiers as a prostitute. She chose to live.

After liberation, I returned to the Van Tol home.

The place was beyond recognition. It had turned into a filthy brothel, with several grimy prostitutes hanging about. I was shocked and dejected when Toos seemed to fit right into the scene. She had little to say, offered me a cup of tea, but I refused. I had to get out of there before the memory of the noble Toos, her beautiful tidy home and its warm atmosphere became obliterated by reality.

Later, I ran into Albert. "I don't recognize my wife anymore," he lamented. He revealed that he was moving to Indonesia to get away from his anguish. I never saw either of them again. They had heroically saved our lives and I had to stand by and see the disintegration of theirs.

Benno today among his paintings

After marrying a survivor in 1948, I left Holland and settled in Israel. In 1956, for health and family reasons, we joined a relative in Australia and raised children and grandchildren there.

In 1987, I was invited to participate in the dedication of a monument to the Jewish citizens of Denekamp who perished under the Nazis. It was one of the high points of my life. It brought back memories of the horrors and deprivations we had endured, but, above all, it exemplified the Dutch spirit of love of freedom, tolerance, unselfishness, concern and warmth. No wonder that almost half of those honored as Righteous Gentiles by Yad Vashem, the International Holocaust Museum in Jerusalem, were citizens of Holland.

Abandoned

As told by "Diana Binder"
(pseudonym for a survivor who
wishes to remain anonymous)

WARSAW, POLAND
BROWARD COUNTY, FLORIDA

When the Germans marched into Poland in 1939, I was only three and oblivious to the events that plunged the world into turmoil.

My little cosmos consisted of Mama, Papa, my 13-year-old sister Ruth, my 12-year-old brother Witold, and my 8-year-old brother Janus. We lived in a comfortable apartment in Skarzysko, a small town about halfway between Warsaw and Cracow. Papa had something to do with banking.

We were all excited when, in March 1941, Mama gave birth to a baby boy. I loved his large, sad, deep blue

217

eyes. We named him Henry. I took care of him whenever Mama would allow it. To me, he was a living toy.

Only a few months later, Papa and Janus suddenly vanished from my life. All Jews were ordered into a nearby ghetto. Witold urged Papa not to go, but for whatever his reasons, Papa decided to obey the order, but leave the family behind. Janus pleaded to accompany him and he prevailed. We never saw either of them again.

Witold supported us with his clever bartering. He bought and sold clothing, cigarettes, pots and pans, and anything else we or nearby acquaintances had to spare. He went into the countryside and traded with friendly farmers for bread, sugar and grains for sale or barter in town.

Before the year ended, my sister Ruth was caught in a German dragnet on the street and disappeared. Mama and Witold decided that it had become too dangerous to stay together. With great trepidation, Mama wrapped Henry in a warm blanket and handed him to Witold. They cried together, huddled close to each other, and Witold left with the baby.

He took an early morning train to Cracow and found an orphanage near the station. He placed the baby on the sidewalk near an entrance gate and hid behind a tree across the street. At 7 AM, the caretaker, who came out to sweep the area, found little Henry, carefully picked him up in the blanket and carried him into the building. Witold sighed with relief. At least Henry would be safe for the time being; no one would suspect him of being Jewish since he was not circumcised, and Witold would know where to find him again after the war.

I missed Henry terribly. Whenever I heard a baby cry, I thought it was my little brother. I peeked into every carriage that passed by. I longed for him.

Even at my young age, I was aware there was danger. Germans were all around us, Mama was always crying, Papa and Janus were gone, people were talking about who got killed, there was shooting on the streets, and I instinctively knew to be afraid. Witold slowly and patiently explained to me that I would have to go away for a while and pretend to be someone else. He practiced with me hour after hour to make me comfortable with my story:

My name was Barbara Slasak, I lived in Mielec, was visiting my grandmother in Warsaw and became separated from her and was lost. Above all, I was never to tell anyone I was Jewish.

One day, near Christmas 1942, it was time to say goodbye to Mama. I hugged and kissed her, but I couldn't understand why she cried so profusely. I was simply going on a little trip and would be back soon.

As it turned out, I never saw my dear mother again. After we left, she ventured into the streets and was denounced to the Nazi police by one of her neighbors. The Germans had begun to offer money and food to anyone identifying Jews, and death to those who failed to do so. Upon his return to an empty room, a shocked and frightened Witold escaped to the countryside and, with false papers obtained by barter, hoped to fade into obscurity among the farm hands.

On the train to Warsaw, Witold went over my story again and again. He told me not to speak to him once we had arrived, but to follow him. When he had found a church, he would lift the navy blue student cap he always wore and I would enter that church. He promised to come for me as soon as possible.

I followed him through the snow-covered streets and saw him stop near a large building. He raised his eyes toward its steeples and lifted his blue cap. I took a last look at my older brother, walked to the entrance and pulled on the large metal ring protruding from the mouth of a brass lion as hard as I could until the door opened enough for me to slip in.

I was scared. The church was so big, and the ceiling so high. I felt very alone and forsaken. The quiet intensified my feeling of abandonment. I crowded into the corner of a pew to obscure my presence and watched as people kneeled, prayed and left. As the evening approached, a helper walked along the aisle, checking each row. He found me, smiled and suggested I go home. "I don't know where that is," I said. "Why are you here?" he wanted to know. I told him that I had been playing with some children and came in to hide from them.

The helper called the priest who lived nearby. He was a very friendly man who asked a lot of questions. I answered them exactly as I had learned—my name was Barbara Slasak, I was visiting my grandmother, played with some children, and didn't remember where grandmother lived. The priest took me by the hand and we walked together through the streets near the church, carefully looking at all the houses. Of course, I couldn't identify any.

As darkness fell, the priest took me back to his quarters and I stayed with his maid and cook. I eagerly accepted the delicious dinner and slept soundly. During the following three days, we would walk the streets but, of course, could never find the non-existent house.

On Sunday, the kind priest announced at the service that he had a lost little girl and asked for a volunteer to take me for awhile. That afternoon, a couple came and brought me to their apartment. They fed me, bathed me, washed my hair and took me shopping the following day for clothes. The man was usually silent and gruff at times, but the woman was very warm and loving. They had no children.

Every day they would question me. "Are you Jewish?" I always said no. The Warsaw ghetto was nearby, and people tried to escape all the time. If Poles were caught with a Jewish girl, they were in deep trouble. Every day, the woman would bring me in front of a picture on the wall and ask, "Do you love Mary and Jesus?" "Yes, I do," I would answer. One day several weeks later, she added, "If you love them, tell me the truth. I will not punish you for it and nothing will change. Are you Jewish?" Under this pressure, I finally admitted it. "Then we must get you papers tomorrow," she declared.

The next morning, she took me to the police station and had me sit on a bench while she went into an office. She emerged a while later and told me to stay there while she went home for additional papers. After several hours, a man in high black boots came by and ordered me into his office. I knew the woman would never return. I felt betrayed and abandoned again. Did she turn me in? Did her husband force her to get rid of me? Did the authorities make her attempt at getting papers so difficult that it scared her off? I didn't know.

The man in the boots kept asking me if I were Jewish, and I cried "NO" again and again. Finally he picked up a rubber truncheon and lifted it to beat or scare me. At that moment, a Polish policeman entered, surveyed the scene with disgust and shouted, "Are you crazy? She is only a little girl!" With that, he took my hand and led me out. As we walked, he shared with me the sandwich he was eating. We took a trolley to a social agency which placed children in orphanages. He was very friendly and liked me because I reminded him of his daughter who had recently died, he said.

At the agency, we were brought into an office, and after a whispered conference, the man in charge announced that the agency would accept me. The kind policeman hugged me and promised to come with his wife to visit and take me to his home from time to time. I never saw him again, although after the war I learned that he had indeed tried to visit me but the agency would not reveal where I had been placed.

At the end of the day, the manager of the agency led me by the hand to a trolley which took us to the outskirts of the city. During the ride, he told me that he was Stanislaw Kornacki, a 30-year-old widower who lived with his sister and two nieces in an apartment in Warsaw. He lifted me off the top steps of the trolley and, after a short walk, left me in an orphanage, my new home. He promised to see me on Sundays.

True to his word, Mr. Kornacki came every Sunday for long visits. Later, he took me to his apartment for weekends. There I played with Krysia and Basia, his nieces, and we became close friends. These visits and the warm link to a loving family were in stark contrast to life in the orphanage. Aside from a soft bed and tasty food, Mr. Kornacki and his family gave me what I craved most. They loved me, just me, talked to me, sang to me, tucked me into bed, cuddled me. It wasn't "all you kids take a shower" or "all children go to sleep now," as in the orphanage.

Mr. Kornacki would often tell me that he had written to various social agencies in Poland, but no one reported a missing 6-year-old girl fitting my description. He wanted me to be his daughter, he said, but would continue the search unless I told him not to. I suggested he give it up. He asked me if there were anything that I could add that might help. He assured me over and over again that even if I told him something I considered "terrible," it would not change his love for me. I trusted him, and about four months later finally revealed that I was Jewish. He understood why his efforts had been in vain. As promised, it changed nothing. His warmth had not cooled by even one degree.

Soon, Mr. Kornacki began calling me "daughter" and I responded with "father." It sounded so good. It gave me a feeling of identity and security. Krysia and Basia became my "cousins." This was one of the happiest times of my childhood. From early 1943 until the fall of 1944, I spent my days in blissful boredom at the orphanage, immunized from the cold atmosphere by the anticipation of the weekend with my new family. If there had been room in the apartment, they would have let me move in permanently.

I loved them as sincerely as they loved me. But I never forgot my real family, especially Henry. I still looked at every one-year-old to see if I had found him. In my memory, he always remained that age.

The Polish uprising began in August 1944, as the Red Army approached the Vistula River just east of Warsaw. There had been a secret agreement between Stalin and Polish underground leaders that the Red Army would shell the city as soon as the rebellion began. This would force the Germans off the streets. But the Russian guns were silent. The uprising reached a furious peak after one month, but collapsed without the promised Soviet support. Thousands died on both sides. The Nazis were furious and vowed to burn Warsaw to the ground.

When the uprising began, Father told me he would be unable to visit for a while—he was participating in the revolt. When it ended, the Germans began to put the torch to the city. We were rushed out of the orphanage, lined up in a column, and our teachers were ordered to bring us to a nearby square where others were being assembled for shipment to a concentration camp. Once more, I felt abandoned. Where was Father? Where was I going with the other children? Why didn't he take me away with him? Why didn't he protect me?

One of our teachers talked to several German officers, pleading for mercy, in the name of Christ, for these orphans. Time and again, she was rebuffed, but she persisted until one high ranking officer agreed to help. He wrote something on a piece of paper and handed it to her with instructions. Her group of about 25 would be positioned at the rear of the column. When they approached the railroad tracks, she was to lead the children off the road and wait in nearby bushes until dark. A small cattle train was scheduled to come through the area and would take the group south.

Exactly as the officer had stated, the train blew its whistle as it neared the road. The teacher stepped onto the tracks and waved a white handkerchief until the train came to a halt. The engineer, at first very annoyed, read the note and, with a shrug, motioned to the group to get aboard one of the box cars. It stank from animals and we sat on some straw and breathed slowly until we got used to the stench. Early in the morning, we arrived in Cracow.

Our dauntless teacher went into the city and found a public school building to shelter us. Our tired and hungry column made its way to the site and fell exhausted onto hastily prepared beds and cots. I was nine years old by then and thought I would always be alone, unloved and deserted.

Every day, different families would bring food for all of us. On Sundays, we were assembled in a social hall, where adults would greet us and take us to their homes for the day. It brightened my life but didn't penetrate my loneliness.

One day during class, the teacher told me to go to the dining room where a visitor was waiting for me. Puzzled but obedient, I opened the door of the room and there he stood, Stanislaw Kornacki, my father. For a moment, I lost my breath. Then I ran toward his open arms and kissed his smiling and loving face. We cried and hugged, and I clung to him like metal to a magnet. He was all I had and I loved him.

He had searched everywhere for me in the smoldering rubble around my orphanage and had almost given up hope until he heard that a group of children had arrived in Cracow. On his way to find me, he said, he was robbed by marauders, a common occurrence in those days. "Don't worry, Father," I assured him, "here, you can have these." I handed him the three Groschen (pennies) I had saved and treasured. They were my worldly possessions. He reached for me and hugged me intensely. I felt a tear landing on my cheek.

For two days, it was heaven. We talked, laughed, played, cried, sang and shared our feelings. Then Father announced that he must return to Warsaw. He promised to come for me as soon as he had found a job and housing. I held on to him and would not let go. He took me to dinner in a fancy restaurant and then to the movies. He gave me the address of a friend with whom he was temporarily living and told me to write. When he left the next morning, I was sad, but I knew I was not abandoned. I would never be alone again.

The make-shift eating and living arrangements at the public school lasted a few months. Someone heard about our group and donated a large home in the Tatra Mountains for our use. It was about 60 miles south of Cracow. The patient and kind families gave us a big party, and the following morning we boarded a bus to our new residence in the village of Poronin.

I immediately wrote to Father to inform him of my new address. He was happy to hear that I was among nice people in a pleasant and quiet atmosphere. He was still looking for housing and a permanent position. Meanwhile, he sent me books, candy, many letters and his love.

The war ended four months later. I received word from Father that he had returned to the apartment house where he was born and had spent his youth. It was on the fashionable Aleje Ujazdowskie, the street where most countries maintained their embassies. The front apartments had been destroyed, but the rear apartments, including Father's, were still intact. The Germans who had lived there had fled, so Father took possession. In addition, he had found a job with a publishing firm. So, as promised, he came to Poronin to end my solitary existence. Oh, what a joyous day it was!

The apartment was large. Father's sister, Aunt Julie, stayed with us in the living room. Aunt Sophia and Uncle Roman occupied a bedroom, a young couple with a baby lived in the other bedroom, and later a cousin arrived and slept in the kitchen. It was a bit crowded, but it was full of life, affection, caring and activity. Father put me into one of the remaining schools and I was a happy 10-year-old girl gleefully looking forward to every new day. After a few months, Father made my status official. As no one had claimed me since the war ended, he formally adopted me, obtained a set of identification papers for me, and I legally became what I had been all along—his loving daughter. I loved my father, aunts and cousins and life was once again wonderful. Although I still longed for my baby brother Henry and remembered my real family, I tried not to think of anyone or anything that could intrude on my happiness.

Unknown to me, my brother Witold had survived by working on remote farms, protected by forged papers. As soon as the war ended, he came to Warsaw to search for me. By this time, he was a young man of 18. Unable to find me, he traveled to Cracow, returned to the orphanage where he had left Henry and found the caretaker, who told him that he had turned the baby over to the nuns in the orphanage. When pressed, they told him the baby had died. Witold insisted on seeing the death certificate. When he noticed that it was neither notarized nor signed by a doctor, he demanded an explanation. The nuns simply insisted Henry had died.

Witold returned to Skarzysko where he found an aunt who had survived. With her help, he sold a factory formerly owned by our grandfather and with the proceeds hired an attorney to investigate Henry's fate. After two years of litigation, the courts forced the orphanage to reveal their secret. They had delivered Henry to a family who wanted to adopt him, but only on condition that his whereabouts never be revealed. Witold's attorney brought the couple to court, and, by means of blood tests and old photographs, proved conclusively that the two were indeed brothers. The court granted Witold custody of the 6-year-old boy. Henry clung to his adoptive mother and physically resisted leaving with a brother he had never known. But Witold took him by force. For many weeks, the younger boy would not take off the clothes his parents had given him, barely ate, and yearned to return to the people who had loved him.

During the months of litigation, Witold heard from the Red Cross that our sister Ruth, who had been swooped up in the streets, was alive. She had been imprisoned in various labor camps and happened to be in Berlin when a massive air raid trapped her under the rubble of a building. She suffered severe injuries to her body and face and was hospitalized in Salzburg, Austria.

After the Americans occupied the area, she recovered and worked as a translator for the Captain in charge. They fell in love and the officer took her with him to America, married her, arranged for extensive plastic surgery and provided her with a new face, a new life, and, incidentally, two lovely children. She never gave up the search for her family. When she heard from Witold and Henry, she immediately began preparing the paperwork to bring her brothers to the United States. Although Witold looked forward to seeing Ruth again, he continued searching for me.

One day in the fall of 1947, on my way to school, I felt someone following me. I stood near a shop window and saw the reflection of a young man, eyeing me steadily. I didn't recognize Witold. He had visited many elementary schools in Warsaw and carefully scrutinized each girl to find me. He had been watching me for several days and felt confident that I was his sister. I walked faster toward a bus stop. Father had told me to go near a lot of people if I ever felt in danger. The young man caught up with me and asked, "Are you Barbara Slasak?" How did he know the name my older brother had given me? I responded with fear in my voice, "Yes, I was but I am now Barbara Kornacki." He beamed. "I am your brother Witold," he declared. When I saw him up close, the usual blue student cap on his head and the kind smile on his face, I recognized him. Many thoughts raced through my mind. Oh, my God, what was going to happen now? I wanted him to be alive and find out about my family, but I was so afraid my life would change. I didn't want that to happen. I was so confused.

I continued walking toward school. He wanted me to stay with him, but I told him my father would be upset if I did not attend my classes. Then he stopped me in my tracks with a declaration. "I have Henry!" I was overwhelmed with emotions. "Where is he? How is he?" I asked anxiously. Witold told me briefly how difficult it was to find him and reunite with him. "Come with me," he baited me, "and I will take you to Henry." But I started to leave. He clutched my arm and said sternly, "I can't let you go now. It took me too long to find you and I promised Mama I'd take care of you." I screamed. "Police, police!" A crowd quickly formed and surrounded us. A policeman, on nearby traffic duty, ran over. Witold assured him and the crowd that he was my brother, but I insisted I had never seen this man and that he wanted to kidnap me. The policeman took us both to the station.

A friendly officer questioned Witold privately and then called for me. "Do you have a little brother?" he wanted to know. "Yes," I responded. "And what's his name?" "Henry," I blurted out. So that settled it in the mind of the officer. "Go home and tell your father to come see me," he directed. "I'll give you a letter for him."

I ran to Father's office near our home. He was on the third floor, but I didn't wait for the elevator and flew up the stairs. He saw my excitement and was unable to interpret my garbled chatter. He took me into a small room and calmed me down. I finally caught my breath and told him that my older brother had found me and wanted to take me away. Father turned pale, then white and dropped off his chair onto the floor. I was sure he was dead. Someone had once mentioned that he had a weak heart. I screamed and people in the office revived him. When he felt better, he told me to go to our home while he went to see the officer at the police station.

In the apartment, thoughts of jumping off the balcony crossed my mind. I became very depressed at the possibility of having my 11-year-long life disrupted again. When Father returned, I had only to look at his face to know that all was lost. "Let's get on a train," I pleaded, "and go far away where he will never find us." Father gently insisted that we would have to do what we could legally. "I'll go to court," he promised "and try to get you back."

Two days later, Witold came for me. I took a small satchel with clothes, left my toys and books there for my return, and said many tearful and melancholy goodbyes. My brother took me by train to the orphanage in Czestochowa, where Henry was being cared for. The people there were kind and gentle. They fed us and we relaxed from the long journey. Then Witold took me to the infirmary downstairs where several children were napping on narrow beds and cots. He challenged me. "Go see which one is your brother Henry." I went from bed to bed and found him. I had for the last six years remembered him as small but with large penetrating blue eyes. And there he was, but with fear and unhappiness clouding his face. He did not recognize me and would not come to me. He covered his face with a blanket to shut out the world. We both wanted to be back with the only families we really knew.

Father visited me in Czestochowa and told me he had hired a lawyer to see if he could regain custody. While he was there, it was wonderful. After he left, I would cry for days. He sent me packages of candy, pears, apples and other goodies. My aunts sent me shoes and clothes.

I developed symptoms of tuberculosis and was sent to a sanitorium for two months. I wrote Father many letters, especially complaining that they did not allow me to have a prayer book. Father had taken me to church regularly and I studied all the rituals and took Communion. I liked religion. Witold, however, admonished me for participating in Christian prayers in school. I was 12 years old and didn't know where I belonged.

While recuperating, I heard about a group called Hanoar, Hebrew Youth Organization, from other Jewish girls and joined them at meetings. There I learned about Israel and how important it was for young people to go there. I began to feel comfortable about my Jewishness.

When my stay in the sanitorium ended, I returned to Czestochowa and the routine of my life. I continued my letters to Father. After six months, I developed another spot on my lungs and returned to the sanitorium. I also continued to go to Hanoar meetings and became keenly interested in Israel. When Witold informed me that we would all emigrate to America, I insisted we go to Israel instead. "We'll talk about it after you get well," he promised.

Twice, I had to return to the sanitorium for three months at a time. Eventually, I recovered and was discharged. Witold enrolled me in a camp where young people were being trained for life in Israel. In the fall of 1949, the three of us emigrated to the new Jewish state.

There, I immersed myself in life on a Kibbutz, studied the Bible, learned Hebrew and focused my thoughts on Judaism. My letters to Father, which continued until

"Diana" taking Communion

he died several years later, became fewer and their contents more general. When the salutation changed from "Dear Father" to "Dear Mr. Kornacki," I think he knew that his little girl had found her kismet.

At 20, I married a survivor, had two children and moved to the U.S. to join my sister, Ruth. Henry had preceded me and Witold followed six months later.

In a way, I have led three lives. Each has left indelible entries in the crossword puzzle of my being.

The Man in the Black Car

As told by Olga "Oli" Altman Spitzer Solti

BUDAPEST, HUNGARY
MIAMI BEACH, FLORIDA

The political tensions dominating the European continent in the late 1930s were swept from my mind by thoughts of love for Ignatz Spitzer. I didn't like his first name, so I named him "Koma," a Hungarian term of endearment. My fiancé had a middle management position with a large Swiss international import-export firm in Budapest. As the clouds of war darkened, the firm offered to help its Jewish employees leave the continent. Koma was chosen to go to Argentina to determine how twenty families could best be resettled there. We decided to mix business with pleasure, so we married on January 4th, 1939 and left that night for a honeymoon in Argentina.

After consultations with the firm's representatives and various government officials in Buenos Aires,

Koma concluded that it would be best to organize a cooperative farm to provide shelter and employment for the families while they became acclimated to life in South America. When the plan was proposed to the employees in Europe, it was turned down. The workers were reluctant to relinquish their comforts, good schools, fine restaurants, competent medical services and convenient beauty parlors for the unknown, halfway around the globe.

We decided to remain in Argentina. Koma qualified for a "green card" permitting him to work and obtained a job in sales. We lived in modest comfort. In September 1939, after the inferno of war had been kindled, the Hungarian Embassy notified us that the last ship for Hungary would sail the following month. If we were interested in returning, it was "now or never."

After much agonizing, we decided to return. We felt we would be deserting our families and, as it was, Hungary was not really involved in the conflict and probably would be safe.

Koma's former job had been filled, but his prior Swiss employer found another position for him outside the capital. After several months, he was relocated to Budapest. We lived in a small one-bedroom apartment, happy and in love, and rejoiced in the birth of our daughter Agi in June 1941.

For the next two years, Hungary's national life continued normally while death and destruction rampaged the continent. The government, sensing a Nazi victory, aligned itself with Germany. Hitler's armies crushed most of Europe and his carnage against the Jews was in full swing. The smoke stacks of

Auschwitz, Treblinka and Majdanek spewed their grisly ashes over the countryside without pause. In April 1943, the Nazis turned their attention to their Hungarian allies and demanded that they intern their Jews. The government complied.

Koma was sent to a labor camp about eighty miles west of Budapest, but he was allowed to write letters, and to send and receive packages. I remained in the apartment with Agi until the Germans, betraying their ally, swooped into Budapest in March 1944. I was ordered to vacate my apartment and move in with another woman, a former Jew who had converted. Her husband and Koma were in the same labor camp, ate the same food, absorbed the same abuse, but he wore the white armband of a convert rather than the yellow one of a Jew. To a Nazi it was "once a Jew, always a Jew."

Within three months, the Hungarians had integrated their anti-Semitism with that of the Germans. I was ordered to leave my area and find shelter in the "Jewish section," where each apartment building displayed a large yellow star on its facade. Most were five-story structures, jammed to capacity with Jewish women and children. My sister, whose tiny quarters were too small to accommodate us, persuaded a neighbor to let us move into her second bedroom.

One morning, a Hungarian soldier, blaring over a loudspeaker, ordered all able-bodied women to assemble in front of the building for transportation to labor camps. As we scurried about, it began to rain heavily. The soldier, not anxious to get soaked, rescinded his order and told us to return to our apartments. I real-

ized the ax was about to fall and resolved to do something to save my daughter and, if possible, myself.

I had heard that the Swedish Embassy represented
Argentine interests in Hungary, and also that many
Jews had obtained a Schutzpass (protection pass) from
the Swedes, which was being honored by the Germans.
An embassy official named Raoul Wallenberg, it was
said, was sympathetic to Jews and vigorously intervened on their behalf whenever he could. He would
claim that the persons involved had been granted visas
for immigration to Sweden and were therefore under
the protection of the Swedish Embassy while waiting
for transfer to their new country.

I took Agi and went to the Swedish Embassy. After
a long wait, I was directed to an officer. No—the fact
that we possessed an Argentine green card could not
help us in Budapest. No—he could not simply issue a
Swedish Schutzpass. Agi began to cry when she saw
tears rolling down my cheeks. "Please, Sir," I begged,
"if you can't give me a Schutzpass, give one to my little girl. I want one of us to survive." He must have
been moved. He gave me instructions. "Bring me small
pictures that can be put on a pass and complete the
proper form I will give you. Then come back and I will
see what I can do. You need only one form for yourself and your little girl." With that he reached toward
a small stack of papers. On the spur of the moment I
added, "And one for my husband, please." He handed
me two.

I rushed home and rummaged through all of my
belongings until I found the pictures. I sent a "Rapid
Mail" letter to Koma at the labor camp and implored
him to sign and return the form immediately. A few

days later, with Agi and the two completed papers and pictures in hand, I returned to the compassionate officer. It took a half hour, and I left the building with a Schutzpass for me and Agi, and another for Koma. I was on cloud nine. It was September 29, 1944 that someone helped, someone cared.

The following week, the Hungarian soldier who had avoided the rain returned to assemble a contingent for slave labor. He ordered everyone to report to the countryside within 30 minutes. I carried my newly acquired document and showed it to the soldier, pointing out that I was under the protection of the Swedish Embassy. He cursed and accused me of having a fake pass. I argued with him, loudly proclaiming that the document was genuine. An officer approached to investigate the commotion. He examined the Schutzpass and declared it to be valid. I was permitted to return to my room.

A week later, the loudspeaker blared again, ordering those with Swedish passes to report downstairs with their belongings. We met with thirty women outside the building. The group was marched in columns of two through the streets toward a high apartment building brightly decorated with the Swedish flag, a yellow cross lying sideways on a field of light blue. On the way, Hungarian anti-Semites spat at and cursed us, with fists clenched in anger.

At the Swedish "Safehouse," we received food and were crowded into apartments with others. Actually, with Budapest under constant air bombardment, we spent much of our time in the cellars.

Late in December 1944, a Hungarian police officer appeared at the "Safehouse" and blared an order

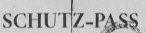

for all able-bodied adults to report outside within five minutes. I dared to ask him where he was taking us. He responded with venom in his voice: "You are not going to hell—yet." I left my daughter with an old woman and joined the others in front of the building. Several trucks were parked, ready to receive the human cargo. We were herded onto the trucks until each was filled to capacity.

Suddenly, a long black car, flying small Swedish flags above its headlights, pulled in front of the trucks, blocking their exit. A tall, handsome man in a dark, belted coat emerged. I had heard about him and now looked on with fascination and awe as Raoul Wallenberg, standing straight as a mighty oak, engaged the Hungarian police officer in earnest conversation. I could not hear what was said, but sensed the tension, confusion and fear in the bearing of the officer. Wallenberg's tone would rise slightly but strongly enough to override any attempt by the officer to contest a point. At the conclusion of the monologue, Wallenberg stood silently, his eyes locked onto those of the officer. My inner excitement made me dizzy. I could hear my heart thump in anticipation. The officer hesitated for a few moments and seemed to come to a decision. He took one step backward, saluted and turned to the truck drivers. "Let them go," he ordered. As I climbed off the rear of the vehicle, I saw the sleek black car drive off, the outline of a well-shaped head visible through its rear window. It was a magical moment I would never forget. It was like a dam, halting the dangerous waters about to drown us. We were safe.

My luck held. Two days later, I met an acquaintance on the street. She greeted me with excitement. "You know, don't you, that your husband is in town?" she asked. I could not believe my ears. The last time I had seen him, he had come to Budapest under escort to complete some task he was assigned. He had been billeted in a large building used by the administrators of the labor camps and was able to visit us once in the house with the yellow star. He did not know, of course, that we were in the Swedish "Safehouse." I had to get to him.

The following day, I dressed myself and Agi in the best clothes we had. I arranged for the 14-year-old daughter of our superintendent to accompany us. Since Jews were allowed on the streets only between 12 and 2 o'clock, anti-Semites sometimes made a special effort to harass pedestrians during those hours. The teenager was under instructions to walk off with Agi in case I encountered any difficulties.

The 30-minute walk to the building was uneventful, except for the anticipation that gripped me. Agi chattered child talk with her companion. There were many Jews from various labor camps, here on special assignment, loosely supervised by Hungarian soldiers.

I didn't see Koma. I approached a group of men, asking if they knew my husband. One pointed behind me. "There he is," he said. I turned and spotted him on top of some stairs, descending with a soldier. He had grown a mustache and was even more handsome than I had remembered him. Agi yelled, "Apu, Apu!" Her daddy's face changed from instant shock, surprise and astonishment to indisputable glee and love. He took the stairs by twos and enveloped us in a strong embrace. It felt wonderful to be crushed by those loving arms. We brought each other up to date and I gave him the Swedish Schutzpass I had obtained for him earlier. I urged him to show it to his guard at once. After a short visit, the curfew was nearly upon us and we had to return. It was a joyous departure. My heart was filled with love and hope.

Koma joined us at the Swedish "Safehouse" two days later. The Schutzpass was the key that opened the

Oli Solti in 1955

gate of his prison. This time my husband was with me when we fled to the cellars during air raids. It made it almost bearable—but not for long. On January 4, 1945, a Hungarian policeman ordered everyone out. We had heard that, with the Red Army surrounding the city, other buildings had been emptied, their occupants marched to the Danube and executed on its banks. The bodies were shoved into the murky waters. Koma was certain that this was the fate awaiting us.

We only took a couple of down pillows to keep Agi warm. Under police escort, we were marched in a direction away from the Danube and led to the Jewish section which had become the Budapest ghetto.

We remained there under barbarous conditions until the Red Army tightened the noose and liberated our area two weeks later.

At this point, Raoul Wallenberg belongs to history. But his few minutes in front of a building in Budapest belong to me. I will preserve his memory to my final day. He was an angel of life.

Friendship

As told by Sarah Steinberger

BUCHAREST, ROMANIA
MIAMI BEACH, FLORIDA

I was too young to understand the events that were overpowering my family, my country Romania and all of Europe. As a little girl of four, I didn't know that my father worked as a forced laborer, clearing the streets of snow, carrying heavy furniture and performing other menial tasks. I thought he still owned his trucking firm that took him from the house at 5 in the morning and returned him at 11 at night.

Romania was an ally of Nazi Germany and had army units fighting against Russia. The Romanians had a German king, Michael of the House of Hohenzollern, and the Nazis relied on him to "take care of" his Jews.

Jews from the Bessarabia and Bukovina regions

were sent to labor and concentration camps in Transnistria. At first, the Jews of Bucharest were not harassed. The men were assigned to forced labor but lived at home. There were designated hours during which a Jew could shop for food.

As their German allies victoriously swallowed most of Europe, Romanian participation in anti-Jewish acts became bolder. Businesses were confiscated, citizens shunned their Jewish friends and acquaintances. Periodically, Jews were rounded up and sent to distant camps.

Our street was "integrated." There were a few Jewish intellectuals and businessmen, Turkish merchants, a Greek shoemaker, and even one family from the German minority that had lived in Romania for generations. Most were financially secure.

The German family, directly across the street, consisted of Wilhelm Hedwig, his wife Mitzi, and two daughters, Grete and Marianne, whom we called "Manni". She was five, one year older than I. We would look at each other from behind the fences of our yards, wishing that we could play together. One day, after obtaining her mother's permission, she invited me and my sister Sonia, a year younger than I, to come over and see her dolls. My mother had no objection so we began to spend time with the Hedwigs.

Manni was a blue-eyed, auburn-haired beauty with a tiny turned-up nose and a pouting mouth. Her sister Grete, already ten, watched our play with tolerant amusement. As we children formed a bond with each other, the adults became friends. Both fathers were named Wilhelm, so we referred to one as "Onkel" Willy, and to the other as "Tata" Willy.

My father spoke German fluently. He had been raised in an area in the north which was once part of the Austro-Hungarian Empire. He had developed a profitable trucking business and was considered to be in the upper middle class. Fearing the worst as the flames of war devoured the Continent, he disassembled several trucks and stored the parts in various junkyards and warehouses belonging to colleagues with whom he had done business over the years and could trust. He reasoned that, when he reassembled them, the trucks could give him a new start after the war. He was absolutely right.

"Onkel Willy" worked in an elegant delicatessen shop, the German-owned Rockhus. Often, he would bring cold cuts, frankfurters, butter and cheese to us to supplement the meager rations we were able to purchase. Of course we reimbursed him. His wife, "Tante Mitzi," fed me and my sister snacks while we played at her house. She also shopped for us, obtaining food items which would be sold out by the time the hour designated for Jewish shoppers arrived. It was strictly forbidden to buy food for Jews, but these dear people ignored the risk.

German officers frequently came to Bucharest. They were usually housed with German families. When they came to the Hedwigs, "Tante Mitzi" would send me home but would allow my blond sister to continue to play there. My dark curly hair looked too Jewish.

In the Spring of '44, the policeman who patrolled our neighborhood approached my father as he returned from his forced labor. They greeted each other cordially. Over the years, my father had greased this man's palm many times, as was customary in Romania. "Mr. Steinberger," the policeman said, "I suggest that you and your family arrange not to be at home tomorrow night. There will be a roundup of Jews, and this area is included." My father thanked him sincerely and slipped him a large banknote. On the wage scale of a slave laborer, it was a very generous gesture. The policeman continued his patrol.

Later, as they were ending the long day with a cup of hot cocoa, Father mentioned this warning to Willy Hedwig. Immediately, our neighbor invited us to sleep in his garage "until the danger passes." "They will never look in a German home for Jews," he assured Father with a smile. It was a spontaneous, sincere and honest invitation, as if he asked us to stop by for cake and ice cream. There seemed to be no concern about the personal risk this represented to his family.

We remained in the Hedwig garage for several days while the Jews in the area were being rounded up for shipment to Transnistria. After that, it was no longer safe to remain in Bucharest.

My father paid one of his former colleagues, a trustworthy trucker, to smuggle the four of us out of Bucharest at night and take us to Draganeasca, a gypsy village about 44 miles to the west. There we rented a small apartment and lived as Christians until the Red Army knocked Romania out of the war in August 1944. We then returned to our house in Bucharest.

The Russians decided to begin rebuilding their country with labor from conquered lands. They arrested all German citizens, using the excuse that "they must have been collaborators." Willy Hedwig was

among those sent to the giant Donbas coal mines as slave laborers.

My father reassembled the few trucks he had hidden before the war and resumed business activities. We children played and visited with each other, just as in the "old" days a few months ago.

Suddenly, Manni came down with a severe fever and stiffness of the neck. A doctor diagnosed it as meningitis. "Tante Mitzi" was frantic. Only the newly discovered penicillin could save her little girl. The new miracle drug was impossible for the doctor to find and, besides, it was too expensive for her to afford.

My father took everything he had saved and searched for the wonder drug in the only place where anything could be found for a price—the black market. For an exorbitant sum, he obtained an American oil-based penicillin which remained potent for 24 hours between injections. It saved Manni's life. She recovered within a week. Mitzi Hedwig had her young child back.

Father considered it a sign from heaven that he had the opportunity to repay, at least in part, the many kindnesses the Hedwig family had extended to us at great peril to themselves.

Epilogue:

Willy Hedwig was released from the Soviet coal mines five years later. He was shunned by many. Association with a former inmate of a communist labor camp could have been dangerous. In the early 1970s, he moved his family to Munich, where he died shortly thereafter from natural causes.

At age 41, Manni became ill and died suddenly. An autopsy revealed a congenital brain defect.

After applying for a visa to Israel in 1958, my father was interned in labor camps for 9 years, accused of "Zionist activities." The authorities wanted to expropriate his house and trucks. To increase their psychological pressure upon him, they interned my mother in a labor camp for two years while they "investigated her participation in Zionist activities." She was released in 1963.

Sonia and I remained as squatters in one barely furnished room in our home, which had been confiscated by the communist government. We survived with the help of the American Joint Distribution Committee and packages from Jewish groups in New York.

After Israel and Romania established diplomatic relations in 1968, my parents were among those whom the Jewish state negotiated to ransom for cash from the Romanian government. They spent the rest of their lives in Israel.

In 1966, I came to America to seek help and funds to bribe my family out of Romania. The state of Israel beat me to it. I remained in New York and obtained a professional degree at Columbia University.

My sister Sonia settled, and still resides, in Massachusetts, and raised a family.

Grete Hedwig lives in Munich, Germany. We correspond regularly and talk occasionally on the telephone. She recently reported that her mother, my "Tante Mitzi," was in an old age home and severely ill.

Desperate Voyage

As told by Terry Wolf

LUXEMBOURG, LUXEMBOURG
WEST PALM BEACH, FLORIDA*

When my mother died in 1931, I was a blossoming young woman of 18, a graduate of Nuremberg High School and a year of finishing school for girls. My father had a busy medical practice, so I took care of the household.

In 1938, I married my cousin Martin in Luxembourg. He had a responsible position in a firm, owned by a German Jew, which dealt with trading and shipping of ore and metals, a highly specialized business. We lived blissfully in an eight-room Luxembourg villa.

As is customary in Europe, we took our vacation in late August. It was 1939. Martin attended to some

*Acknowledgment is made to Holocaust Survivors of West Palm Beach.

business on the French Riviera, and that's where we were, basking in the sun, when the Nazis plunged the world into war.

Martin realized that a return to Luxembourg was unrealistic, so we settled in a residential hotel in Limoges, a small town deep inland and far away from border areas or potential targets.

Although we had obtained our "first papers" for eventual Luxembourg citizenship, we still carried our German passports bearing the large "J" for Jew. But to the French, the "J" made little difference. They rounded up all males with German passports and sent them to an internment camp near the road to Avignon. We deliberately maintained a low profile and rarely ventured out of the hotel. This may have been why the French police somehow missed Martin during the initial round-up. But his luck ran out in November when his secretary sent him a telegram from Luxembourg. It alerted the authorities. They picked him up and sent him to the camp.

While confined, Martin wrote to me regularly and included many business instructions to be forwarded to his office in Luxembourg and to the United States, where the Jewish owner had immigrated in 1936. He conscientiously tried to do his job from his barracks. After four months, the French authorities, possibly by censoring mail leaving the internment camp, realized that Martin could be of significant value to the war effort as an expert in metallurgy. They transferred him to Tours in central France, issued identity papers declaring him a "Prestataire," (a non-combatant civilian in the service of France), and installed him in an office.

Martin's boss in America, understanding the

plight of his Jewish employees, paid for a visa to the Dominican Republic to be issued to us in Paris. The firm's Luxembourg office forwarded this information to Martin. With great joy, Martin and I met in Paris to keep an appointment on April 18, 1940 with the ambassador of the Dominican Republic. He was a charming elderly man who seemed to take a strong liking to me. He had the visa stamped on our French identity papers, wished us luck, and invited me to stop by anytime I would visit Paris. After a few days of bliss, Martin departed for Tours, and, as required, I reported back to the police in Limoges upon my return.

I had barely settled back into my routine when an order was posted for all women without children, carrying German passports, to report at the end of the week for internment in a nearby camp.

As a wife of a Prestataire, I should have been exempt. After all, my husband was in the service of France. The local police commissioner, however, made no such distinctions. To him, a German was a German. When I wrote Martin about it, he complained to his commanding officer, who sent a telegram advising the police commissioner that he had no right to intern the wife of a Prestataire. The commissioner was furious that a military person dared to interfere in a civilian matter. In retribution, he ordered me sent to Gurs, an internment camp for women near the French-Spanish border in the Pyrenees.

Gurs, which later became a concentration camp, housed over 15,000 women, mostly Jews. We were not mistreated, only confined in large barracks, guarded by Moroccan troops. There was little food. I lost 40 of my 127 pounds in the five weeks I was there. I resembled a walking skeleton.

One morning, after a transport had arrived from Luxembourg, I was surprised to find Martin's mother in the barracks next to mine. We had a warm reunion. Martin's father had left her years ago to marry her closest friend. As the fates arranged it, a few days later I spotted that very woman in another barracks, separated from ours by a barbed wire fence.

When the French government capitulated to the Germans in June 1940, all Prestataires were released so they could save themselves. A woman I knew from Limoges who now lived near Gurs learned through a friend who worked with Martin that he was on his way to Gurs to find me. At the same time, the camp commander decided to release all of the inmates. His conscience would not let him turn thousands of innocent women over to the Germans. As the exodus of women began, my mother-in-law and I decided to wait in the camp for Martin. Within a week he arrived. It was a heart-warming reunion. He looked so handsome as he hugged me and his mother and showered us with kisses.

Fortunately, we found a bus which brought us to the station in time to catch the last train to Bordeaux. This seaport on the Bay of Biscay feeding into the Atlantic Ocean was a natural destination for desperate people. It represented the last hope of leaving the continent by ship. After an apprehensive trip, we arrived in the town square in Bordeaux. It was a rainy night, and thick fog blanketed the area, turning it into a domain of darkness and silence. Sometimes we could hear muffled steps as blurry figures passed by, happy that their soft verbal exchanges were in French and not German. As a military truck crawled through the fog, Martin stopped it and pleaded with the driver to give him a lift to the nearest military installation so he could find shelter and food for us. The driver agreed and Martin told us to remain in the square until he returned.

We sat on our suitcases, forlornly staring into the fog and rain, waiting for Martin. Two French women passed by, took pity on us and invited us to come with them for some food. I was delighted. I asked my mother-in-law to remain there with the suitcases and wait for Martin. I would be back with food as soon as possible. She nodded, probably too frightened to say anything.

The women led me along tall narrow houses on a cobblestone street. We entered one. It was such a splendid sensation. For the first time in a year, I felt the warmth and intimacy of a home—it was just wonderful. They served me hot soup, bread and wine. A full course gourmet dinner would have paled in comparison.

Suddenly we heard loud noises in the street. Martin was banging on doors and shouting my name. He could not obtain help and had returned to the square. His mother was unable to tell him where I had gone.

The friendly women sheltered us for the night, and very early in the morning showed us the way to the harbor. "Hurry," they urged, "the Boche (German) is only ten miles away."

There were many people at the waterfront. We learned that Italy had just declared war against France and all shipping had stopped. The waters were mined and Nazi U-Boats prowled the seas. A few small fishing boats were still anchored. We went from one to another, begging for passage out of Bordeaux, but were refused. We joined others who congregated near the empty wharf next to the Administration building, sharing their despair and hopelessness.

Unexpectedly, from the south entrance to the harbor, a small freighter edged its way toward us and tied up at the wharf. The KILISSI was deep in the water, its cargo of green bananas from Africa spilling over on its decks. The captain, a handsome man in his 40s, leaned over the railing, incredulously observing the scene on the dock. About 600 people were pleading, crying, urging and offering bribes to be taken out of France.

The captain seemed deep in thought. Suddenly, he stood erect. He appeared to have come to a decision. He disembarked, made his way through the crowd to the Administration building, remained there for several minutes, and reboarded his ship. He talked earnestly to the crew. Then, every sailor raised his hand. The captain smiled and turned to us. As we learned later, he had asked for and obtained permission from the authorities to attempt to save us, at the risk of his ship, his life and that of any of his crew who voted to come along. In a loud but gentle voice, the captain announced to the hushed crowd that he would make room on the ship and take us out. There was a tremendous cheer and great excitement.

The crew hurriedly threw the bananas into the water—there was no time to unload them. They worked without stop until the hold was cleared and just enough bananas were kept for food on our trip.

With a broad smile on his strong face, the captain shouted to us: "Allons nous, mes enfants." (Let's go, my children.) As we began to board, the sound of gunfire lured our attention toward the horizon.

A German military column was moving snake-like on a narrow road from an elevated area toward the harbor. We streamed up the gangplank and filled every empty inch of the vessel. As soon as the boarding was completed, the ship slowly started underway. We could see Nazi motorcycles racing toward us, gunfire spitting from their sidecars.

The captain told his frightened passengers he would sail very close to the shore to avoid detection and floating mines, and would attempt to make it past Spain into Portugal, a neutral nation.

We had not even left the harbor when the ship's engines suddenly stopped. Six hundred hearts must have done the same. We could again hear the gunfire directed toward us from shore. Had we been inter-cepted by the Germans? Most of the passengers were in the hold, unable to see anything. I was on deck and soon understood why we had stopped. Two men and a woman were following us in a rowboat, screaming to attract our attention. They had, somehow, been overlooked. The captain picked them up and saved them. They hugged those of us on deck and were grateful not to have been abandoned. The woman, a registered nurse, became one of my closest friends.

Many people were in poor health before they came on board. The banana diet made more people ill. The choppy waters, the gray foreboding waves and the terri-ble apprehension about the outcome gripped everyone aboard. When the water supply ran out, we switched to wine. But this was wine to exist, not to enjoy.

Finally, the great moment arrived. We approached Lisbon. This meant freedom, food, water and medical help. It meant a chance to cable friends, arrange visas to safe havens, to breathe freely without tension and danger.

How wrong we were. The Portuguese authorities refused us food, water or medical help. Our captain pleaded on our behalf, but to no avail. After several hours, we were told that we would leave the freighter and be transferred via an open ferry to a large Morocco-bound French warship anchored nearby in the harbor.

It was a sorrowful scene. We disembarked from the ship, thanking any crew member in sight, tears rolling down our faces, and boarded the ferry. We began to sing the *Marseillaise,* our voices swelling as the ferry filled to capacity. Our beloved captain, his face white and fighting tears, stood on the bridge, his right hand in a stiff salute. He remained rigid in that position as distance began to diminish our vision. Soon he disappeared from sight.

Subsequent events entailed many tribulations that we had to endure before we finally came to America. But I will leave that for another time because I don't want to detract from the story of a gallant man to whom the value of human life meant more than bananas, profit, comfort and personal safety. Whenever his final voyage, I hope it is to Paradise.

Terry—a few years ago

Fish Hooks and Nets

As told by Basia Gross Lederman

WARSAW, POLAND
MIAMI BEACH, FLORIDA

There probably were few Jews in the early 1900s who imported goods from Japan to Poland. Maybe my grandfather was the only one. As a young man, supporting a wife and three children, he was employed in a business in Warsaw that sold Japanese fish hooks and nets. After his wife was killed in an accidental fall, he married the owner's only daughter, who helped him raise the children with love and devotion. When her father died, he left the business to his son-in-law, my grandfather, Samuel Gross.

My father worked in the business as a youngster, completed his education, and married my mother. I was born in the winter of 1937.

Two years later, the Nazi conquest of Poland

changed everything. The Warsaw ghetto was being prepared to confine the area's Jews. Grandfather and Father realized they had to do something quickly to protect the large quantity of Japanese merchandise they had stored. Like everyone else, they believed the war would end soon and we would resume our normal lives.

Grandfather approached a friendly competitor, a Mr. Warszawski, a devout Polish Catholic who could be trusted to keep his word, and requested that he allow Grandfather to store merchandise in his warehouse. If he ran short and needed some items, Mr. Warszawski was welcome to them. When the war ended, the stored items would be returned to Grandfather, together with any monies they had generated. Mr. Warszawski agreed and the transfer was made.

Day by day, the situation deteriorated. The Germans rounded up Jews in the streets and took them away to unknown fates. People simply disappeared. My mother, who had many friends, found someone who, for a substantial sum, provided her with forged Polish identity papers which changed her into Anna Kaminska, a Catholic peasant woman. With her fair hair and blue eyes, she could easily pass as a gentile. My father, on the other hand looked too Jewish to attempt this subterfuge.

We went into hiding immediately after my grandparents were caught in a Nazi roundup and disappeared. One of Mother's friends took us in. At the risk of her life, she housed and fed us for several weeks. But it became too dangerous as German soldiers began to search aggressively for Jews. For several months, we lived in a "Christian" apartment which Mother was

Basia and mother in hiding

able to rent with her false papers. Father and I remained indoors while Mother occasionally ventured out to secure food. One day, she was recognized in the street by a former neighbor. We could not risk the possibility of betrayal and fled the apartment, taking only valuables that could easily be carried and converted to cash. Everything else was left behind.

Mother's kind friend had some elderly relatives who lived on a farm on the outskirts of Grodzisk-Mazowiecki, a village about 20 miles southwest of Warsaw. Theirs would be the ideal hiding place. Not only were they poor and needed what money we could pay, but they lived in social as well as physical isolation. They were gruff, grumpy, hostile and difficult to get along with. They disliked the villagers, and the feeling was mutual. No one ever came to visit. Their young daughter, Stefa, had left to settle in Warsaw and it was rumored that she had formed a romantic liaison with a German officer. This ostracized the couple even more.

It was perfect. Mother's friend made the arrangements for us. We lived in one room and shared the kitchen and the outhouse with the elderly couple. I can't recall that we ever conversed or socialized with our landlords. My parents admonished me not to speak to anyone, not to cry, to stay away from windows and other people. I thought this was a normal lifestyle.

It was impossible to go into the village because strangers would be noticed immediately. My mother was the only one with papers that allowed her freedom of movement. She would take the train to Warsaw and return with food and other necessities she was able to purchase. While she was away, Father taught me language, mathematics, history, and other subjects I would have studied in school.

Our money began to run out. On her next trip to Warsaw, Mother visited the Polish competitor who was harboring Grandfather's supplies. Identifying herself as the daughter-in-law of Mr. Gross, she informed him that Mr. Gross had disappeared and must be presumed dead, and that she needed money to exist. The man was terribly upset.

"You are crazy to come here," he shouted. "I don't want to be seen with you. Go away." "I will not," my mother responded. "I have a daughter and a husband and I won't let them die. You have to help me." "What do you want from me?" he pleaded. In a firm tone she replied, "Sell our merchandise little by little along with yours, and I will come once a month to get some money so I can pay the people where I live." The merchant asked, "What will I do when Mr. Gross returns and wants his merchandise or his money?" Mother assured him that this would not happen and added, "Don't you see what is going on?" Mr. Warszawski capitulated.

Each month, Mother would come to collect money from the reluctant merchant. He was frightened, knowing that he could be shot if caught helping a Jew.

An unexpected event occurred on the farm where we were hidden. The couple's daughter suddenly returned with a baby. Apparently, the rumors had been correct. We expected it would endanger our refuge, with men coming and going to buy the young woman's sexual favors. But she was shunned for having carried a German child and no one came around. I had to share my bed with her, but we had no other contact. She kept to herself with her baby.

One day, immediately after the Polish uprising in the fall of 1944, Mother came into Mr. Warszawski's shop for her monthly collection. This time, the man seemed happy to see her, smiled and eagerly handed over more than the usual amount. Mother was surprised and pressed for an explanation. He revealed that the warehouse was severely damaged by an explosion during the uprising. All of his goods were burned or destroyed, but the area in which Mr. Gross' merchandise was stored remained untouched. "This is a sign from God!" he exclaimed. "To help you is the right thing to do." He promised he would never again make it difficult for her to receive her money. And he kept his promise.

Basia and mother (now deceased) in 1984

We stayed on that farm for two years until the Red Army liberated the area. We had had enough of Poland. Mother sold the remaining stock of fish hooks and nets to Mr. Warszawski for a modest sum. We then moved to Lampertheim, Germany where we settled in a camp organized to help Jewish survivors emigrate to other countries, and eventually made contact with relatives in Colombia who brought us there. We led a peaceful life. I married a doctor and accompanied him when he moved his practice to the United States.

Occasionally, when I browse leisurely through the aisles of a department store, I shop at the sports counter and pick up packets of fish hooks to see where they are made. I smile when I remember that these little twisted pieces of wire helped our family survive.

Map of Nazi concentration camps

Progression of Evil
A Chronology

1933

January   Hitler becomes chancellor of Germany.

March   First concentration camp established at Dachau for political and criminal prisoners.

              Nazi-dominated legislature passes law suspending civil liberties.

April   Government promotes one-day boycott against Jewish businesses.

              Jews prohibited from working in government offices.

              Nazis outlaw Jewish ritual slaughter.

              Gestapo (secret state police) is established.

May   Books by Jewish authors burned publicly.

September   Jewish employees discharged from broadcasting, the press, theater, literature and music.

October   Germany renounces membership in League of Nations.

1934

August   Paul von Hindenburg, German President, dies. Hitler named President and Commander-in-chief of armed forces.

1935

March	Hitler resumes military conscription, in violation of the Versailles Treaty.
May	Jews barred from service in German armed forces.
September	The Nuremberg Laws—anti-Jewish laws, excluding Jews from becoming German citizens, marrying Aryans, flying the German flag and limiting various forms of contact between Jews and Germans.
November	"Jew" is defined as anyone with three Jewish grandparents, or one with two Jewish grandparents who is married to a Jew or is the child of a Jewish parent.
December	Jews discharged from the Civil Service.

1936

March	Jewish doctors barred from practicing medicine in government institutions.

1937

July	Buchenwald concentration camp is established.

1938

March	German troops annex Austria. All anti-Jewish decrees apply immediately.
April	Jews must register their property with authorities.
June	Jewish doctors permitted to treat only other Jews.
August	Jewish men and women in Germany ordered to add "Israel" or "Sarah" as middle names.
September	Jewish lawyers barred from practice.

October	Passports of German Jews stamped with "J" (Jude).
	Germans expel 17,000 Polish Jews. Poland refuses them entry and interns them at the border.
November	Following the assassination of a consular official in Paris by a distraught Jewish youth whose parents had been deported, Nazis organize a "spontaneous" pogrom in Greater Germany. Synagogues are burned, businesses plundered and destroyed, and about 30,000 Jewish men are shipped to concentration camps. History refers to this night, November 9–10, as The Night of the Broken Glass (Kristallnacht). The Nazis levy a fine of 1 billion Reichsmark on the Jewish community.
	Jewish students expelled from German schools.

1939

January	Jews forbidden to work with Germans.
May	Nazis establish Ravensbrueck concentration camp for women.
	The British government issues The MacDonald White paper, restricting Jewish immigration to Palestine.
September	German army invades Poland. World War II begins.
	Jews throughout Germany forbidden to be out of doors after 8:00 PM.
	The USSR annexes parts of Eastern Poland.
October	Nazis establish the first ghetto in Poland.
	Deportation of Jews in Austria, Germany and Polish cities to designated areas in Poland begins.

| December | All Jews in Poland ordered to wear yellow star. |
| | German government commandeers all Jewish properties in Poland. |

1940

February	The Lodz ghetto is established.
May	Construction of a concentration camp at Auschwitz is completed.
	Himmler suggests to Hitler that the Jews of the occupied areas be relocated to Africa.
	Lodz ghetto, with 165,000 Jews, is sealed off.
	Germany conquers Holland, Belgium and Luxembourg.
June	France surrenders to Germany.
	Italy joins the war against the Allies.
	The USSR occupies Estonia, Latvia and Lithuania.
August	Anti-Jewish decrees are proclaimed in France, Luxembourg, The Netherlands, Belgium, Romania, Hungary, Bulgaria and Slovakia.
November	The Warsaw ghetto, with 500,000 Jews, is sealed off.
	Romania, Hungary and Slovakia join the Berlin-Rome-Tokyo Axis.

1941

| January | Hundreds of Jews slaughtered by Iron Guard during anti-Jewish riots following an unsuccessful coup attempt in Romania. |
| February | Deportations from Holland to Buchenwald begin. |

March	Bulgaria joins the Axis powers.
	The ghetto in Cracow is sealed off.
	Adolf Eichmann is appointed chief of the Jewish Affairs Section of the Gestapo.
April	The Lublin ghetto is sealed off.
	Germans conquer Jugoslavia and Greece.
May	Romania decrees that Jews can be drafted for forced labor.
June	Germany invades the USSR. Closely behind its armies, special mobile killing squads engage in the mass murder of Jews wherever they are found. Under the command of German officers, these squads comprise volunteers from various countries, especially Latvia, Lithuania and Romania.
	Hungary enters the war against the USSR.
July	Ghettos are established in most large cities, its occupants systematically murdered or deported to concentration camps.
September	First experimental gassing takes place on Soviet prisoners of war in Auschwitz.
	Jews in Germany ordered to wear the yellow star.
	34,000 Jews murdered at Babi Yar, near Kiev.
October	All Jewish emigration from Germany ceases.
December	Chelmno extermination camp opens.

1942

January	A Nazi conference in Wannsee, suburb of Berlin, coordinates the "final solution to the Jewish problem," the extermination of all Jews in Europe.

February	First transport of Greek Jews arrives in Auschwitz.
March	The death camp at Birkenau begins operations.
	First transport of French Jews arrives in Auschwitz.
	The first of 600,000 Jews murdered at Belzec death camp.
April	Dutch Jews ordered to wear the yellow star.
May	Sobibor extermination camp begins operations.
June	Jews of Belgium and France ordered to wear yellow star.
July	The first of over 900,000 Jews murdered in newly-opened Treblinka death camp.

1943

January	Jews of the Warsaw ghetto resist deportation. The uprising is quickly and brutally suppressed.
February	First transport of Gypsies arrives in Auschwitz.
April	Jews of the Warsaw ghetto begin armed resistance. For nearly a month, they fight from the sewers and ruins against vastly superior forces. Eventually, the ghetto is leveled by the enraged Germans.
June	Jews in the Czestochowa ghetto revolt against the Germans. They are subdued and deported to death camps.
July	Himmler orders all ghettos in Poland eradicated and Jews to be either used as laborers or liquidated.
August	Uprising in Treblinka death camp is quelled by Nazis.

Uprising in Bialystok ghetto is suppressed.

September   Following an aborted revolt in the Vilna ghetto, many resistance fighters escape and join partisan units.

The Vilna ghetto is destroyed.

October   Danes smuggle over 7,000 Danish Jews to Sweden.

Uprising in Sobibor death camp brutally subdued.

Jews of Rome deported to Auschwitz.

1944

March   Germans occupy Hungary, their ally.

April   Hungarian Jews required to wear yellow star.

May   The first of about 440,000 Hungarian Jews arrive in Auschwitz and are gassed.

July   The Red Army liberates Vilna.

German officers unsuccessfully attempt assassination of Adolf Hitler.

Russians liberate Majdanek extermination camp.

August   Allied forces liberate Paris.

Polish Warsaw uprising begins. Fierce fighting continues until October when the revolt is repressed.

October   In an unsuccessful rebellion in Auschwitz, one gas chamber is destroyed.

1945

January   Auschwitz is ordered evacuated. Death march to other camps begins for over 66,000 prisoners, while about 64,000 others remain to await the next march.

Soviet troops liberate Warsaw.

Red Army liberates Budapest. Raoul Wallenberg is arrested.

Russians enter Auschwitz. Find only 7,650 inmates.

Death march of Stutthof concentration camp victims.

April U.S. troops liberate Buchenwald concentration camp.

Bergen-Belsen camp is liberated by British forces.

Americans liberate Dachau.

Hitler commits suicide in Berlin.

May Soviets conquer Berlin.

Germany surrenders unconditionally to the Allies.

Bibliography

Suggested references dealing with the Holocaust.

Bauer, Yehuda. *A History of the Holocaust.* New York: Franklin Watts, 1982.

Berenbaum, Michael, ed. *A Mosaic of Victims: Non-Jews Persecuted and Murdered by the Nazis.* N.Y. University Press, 1990.

Dawidowicz, Lucy. *The War Against the Jews 1933–1945.* New York: Bantam, 1986.

Friedlander, Albert H. *Out of the Whirlwind.* New York: Schocken Books, 1976.

Gilbert, Martin. *MacMillan Atlas of the Holocaust.* New York: MacMillan, 1982.

Gordon, Sarah. *Hitler, Germans and the "Jewish Question."* Princeton, N. J.: Princeton University Press, 1984.

Hilberg, Raul. *The Destruction of European Jews.* New York: Holmes and Meier, 1985.

Levi, Primo. *Survival in Auschwitz.* New York: MacMillan, 1987.

Morse, Arthur D. *While Six Million Died: A Chronicle of American Apathy.* New York: Overlook, 1983.

Shirer, William L. *The Rise and Fall of the Third Reich: A History of Nazi Germany.* New York: Touchstone, 1981.

Whiteman, Dorit Bader. *The Uprooted: A Hitler Legacy*. New York: Insight Books, 1993.

Wiesel, Elie. *Night*. New York: Bantam, 1984.

Wyman, David S. *The Abandonment of the Jews*. New York: Pantheon, 1984.

Suggested references dealing with courage, rescue and heroism.

Anger, Per. *With Raoul Wallenberg in Budapest: Memories of the War Years in Hungary*. New York: Holocaust Library, 1981.

Atkinson, Linda. *In Kindling Flame: The Story of Hannah Senesh, 1921–1944*. New York: William Morrow, 1985.

Bartoszewski, Wladyslaw. *The Samaritans: Heroes of the Holocaust*. Boston: Twayne, 1970.

Bauminger, Arieh L. *The Righteous Among the Nations*. Jerusalem: Yad Vashem, 1990.

Flender, Harold. *Rescue in Denmark*. New York: Simon & Schuster, 1963.

Frank, Anne. *Diary of a Young Girl*. New York: Doubleday, 1967, Pocket Books, 1953.

Friedman, Philip. *Their Brothers' Keepers: The Christian Heroes and Heroines Who Helped the Oppressed Escape the Nazi Terror*. New York: Holocaust Library, 1978.

Gies, Miep. *Anne Frank Remembered: The Story of the Woman Who Helped to Hide the Frank Family*. New York: Simon & Schuster, 1988.

Goldberger, Leo, ed. *The Rescue of the Danish Jews*. New York: New York University Press, 1987.

Hallie, Philip. *Lest Innocent Blood Be Shed: The Story of the Village of LeChambon and How Goodness Happened There*. New York: Harper & Row, 1979.

Hellman, Peter. *Avenue of the Righteous*. New York: Atheneum, 1980.

Huneke, Douglas K. *The Moses of Rovno*. New York: Dodd, Mead, 1985.

Laqueur, Walter and Breitman, Richard. *Breaking the Silence*. New York: Simon & Schuster, 1986.

Meltzer, Milton. *Rescue: The Story of How Gentiles Saved Jews During the Holocaust*. New York: Harper & Row, 1988.

Noble, Iris. *Nazi Hunter: Simon Wiesenthal*. New York: Julius Messner, 1979.

Opdyke, Irene Gut. *Into the Flames. The Life Story of a Righteous Gentile*. San Bernardino, CA: Borgo Press, 1992.

Perl, William R. *The Four-Front War: From the Holocaust to the Promised Land*. New York: Crown, 1979.

Ramati, Alexander. *The Assisi Underground: The Priests Who Rescued Jews*. New York: Stein and Day, 1978.

Rittner, Carol and Myers, Sondra, ed. *The Courage to Care: Rescuers of Jews During the Holocaust.*

Senesh, Hannah. *Hannah Senesh, Her Life and Diary*. New York: Schocken, 1973.

Tec, Nechama. *Dry Tears: The Story of a Lost Childhood*. New York: Oxford University Press, 1984.

tenBoom, Corrie. *The Hiding Place*. Old Tappan, N.J.: Revell, 1974. New York: Bantam, 1974.

Weinstein, Frida Scheps. *A Hidden Childhood: A Jewish Child's Sanctuary in a French Convent, 1942–1945*. New York: Hill and Wang, 1985.

Yahil, Leni. *The Rescue of Danish Jewry: Test of a Democracy*. Philadelphia: Jewish Publication Society, 1969.

Zuccotti, Susan. *The Italians and the Holocaust: Persecution, Rescue, and Survival*. New York: Basic Books, 1987.